STRONG
Looks Better Naked

STRONG
Looks Better Naked

KHLOÉ
KARDASHIAN

**SIMON &
SCHUSTER**

London · New York · Sydney · Toronto · New Delhi

A CBS COMPANY

First published in Great Britain by Simon & Schuster UK Ltd, 2015
A CBS COMPANY

5 7 9 10 8 6

Simon & Schuster UK Ltd
1st Floor
222 Gray's Inn Road
London WC1X 8HB

www.simonandschuster.co.uk

Simon & Schuster Australia, Sydney
Simon & Schuster India, New Delhi

The author and publishers have made all reasonable efforts
to contact copyright-holders for permission, and apologise for
any omissions or errors in the form of credits given.
Corrections may be made to future printings.

A CIP catalogue record for this book
is available from the British Library

Hardback ISBN: 978-1-47115-646-5
Trade paperback ISBN: 978-47115-653-3
Ebook ISBN: 978-1-47115-648-9

Interior design by Nancy Singer
Cover design by Richard Ljoenes
Jacket photographs and photo insert by Steven Gomillion

Image credits, which constitute an extension of this copyright page, appear on page 219.

Printed and bound by CPI Group (UK) Ltd, Croydon, CR0 4YY

The
journey of
a thousand
miles
begins with
one step.

—Lao Tzu

In loving memory of my father, Robert.

To the loves of my life:
My sisters, Kourtney, Kimberly, Kendall, and Kylie,
my brother, Robert,
my mother, Kris,
and Caitlyn.

Contents

Part 3: HEART

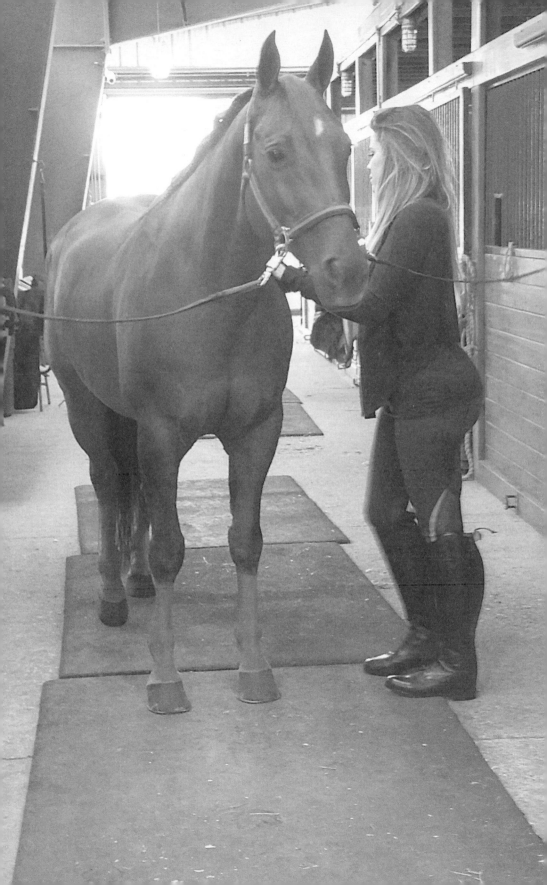

Introduction

Most of my adult life has played out in the public eye. Being on *Keeping Up With the Kardashians* has meant that every significant event in my life has been documented and every insignificant incident has been captured, too. It also means that everything, big and small, has been commented on and speculated about. People gossip about my life over drinks with friends, in office cubicles, on radio shows, and of course in the tabloids, and there are few things tabloids love to talk about more than relationships (especially the end of a relationship) and weight. I can't even count the number of magazine covers that have commented on every change in my body. They write about me when I gain weight and when I lose weight. They come up with crazy explanations for all the changes in my body—from *Khloé must be pregnant* to *Khloé isn't really a Kardashian.*

There are times when living under a microscope can be challenging, but the upside is immense. I have met thousands of inspiring and amazing people along the way, and the connection I feel with them is a great joy in my life. I've also come to realize that, whether I think of myself as a role model or not, there are a lot of young women (and a few men, too) who look up to me. I don't take their *admiration* lightly; it comes with a real responsibility. That is one of the many reasons I wanted to write *Strong Looks Better Naked*.

Even though I've chosen to live much of my life in a fishbowl, I'm a very private person, and while my path to losing weight has received a lot of attention, the emphasis has always been on my body, on what I look like, on how fat or thin I am. But the transformation I have undergone over the last three years is much deeper than shedding a few pounds.

It began when I was going through a particularly hard time in my life—you can read about it on the very first page of the very first chapter. Physically and emotionally I was at a really low point and I needed an outlet. The outlet I discovered was exercise.

At first I focused on my physical body to distract myself from thinking about the things that were causing me real pain. But as my body got stronger, there was an unexpected side effect: My mind became clearer.

Body, mind, soul. That phrase is everywhere; I hear it all the time, but until recently I had never given it much thought. Body. Mind. Soul. What does that even *mean*, anyway? And how many of us actually get beyond *body*?

Ever since I was a little girl, when I first started becoming aware of the world around me, I couldn't help but notice that we judge each other on our looks. That old first-impressions stuff: tall, cute, thin, gangly, chubby, gorgeous, etc.

Later, as we get to know a person, other components come into play. Personality, for example. Grumpy, moody, happy, open, hard to read, etc. And then you dig a little deeper: considerate, thoughtful, selfish, passionate, cold, committed, etc., which further affects the way you see that person. That's why an ordinary-looking woman

can appear stunningly beautiful, because you've gotten to know her, and she's beautiful on the inside. Or conversely, it's why that gorgeous friend looks ugly after you've discovered what she's really like at her core. That's *soul*. That's what I talk about when I talk about *heart*: The essence of a person, her truest self.

But the physical part, the *body*, that's where it all starts. And the way you feel about your body, the way that, ultimately, you *treat* your body, is going to have a huge effect on your mind and your spirit, or as I think about it, your heart.

I began to exercise as an escape, not to change my body, and then my body changed and I can't seem to stop exercising. It is a habit, a very good habit, that keeps me healthy and happy. I found that once I started working hard to improve one element of myself, the quality of my entire life improved dramatically. Not only did I feel more fit and more beautiful, I was also calmer, kinder, more focused and thoughtful, and above all happier.

When I started exercising religiously, I began to talk to friends about it, looking for converts, trying to get them excited about exercise. Most of them wouldn't budge: *I hate exercise. It's too hard. I can't change. I'm big-boned. It hurts too much. I'll always have fat thighs.*

In short, they were defeated by their own thinking. That's the *mind* part. They didn't believe. So they never gave themselves a chance to effect real changes in their lives.

Most of my friends weren't into self-sabotage. The saboteur was the little kid inside them. You know what I'm talking about, that inner child—the small you, the one that refuses to grow up, the one that refuses to take responsibility for anything.

But you can fix that. One thing I've learned from watching my sisters raise their children is that kids need boundaries. They need structure. They need discipline. Without these, they are lost. That's true for all of us.

So when that little voice in your head says, *No, I am not going to the damn gym!* or *Why not have a few more cookies?* you must be firm. Don't cave. You're the boss.

And instead of looking for perfection in yourself, look for *improvement*. Even a tiny forward step is a step in the right direction, no matter how small.

Over the last three years, I've transformed my body, my mind, and my heart. I've never been stronger or happier or more grounded. I hope this book inspires you to build your own form of personal strength. One baby step at a time! That is my philosophy: Small changes and small steps can transform your life.

At the end of the day, it's really quite simple.

Baby steps.

You want to be strong. You have to believe in yourself. True strength comes from looking at yourself with fresh eyes, from having faith, from becoming your own cheerleader. Finding your inner strength is a journey. Nobody else can do it for you.

You want to be healthy. You want to be happy. Be mindful—about the way you approach life, and about the things you can do to change your approach to life.

It is not that difficult. I promise. If you begin with just thirty minutes of exercise a day, the rest of it—mind, heart, spirit—will begin to change.

By now, science has pretty much confirmed that exercise creates powerful changes in our brain. But why rely on science? Find out for yourself.

You deserve an amazing life.

That life is a lot closer than you think.

—Khloé Kardashian
Los Angeles, California
August 16, 2015

Part 1

BODY

Chapter 1
Exercise

When my life was at one of its darkest hours, everything changed—for the better.

At the time, I had been married to Lamar Odom for almost three years, and he'd been through such a challenging summer that he was thinking about taking a break from his pro basketball career. Instead, he powered through and committed himself to the Mavericks, and we found ourselves living in a two-bedroom apartment at the W hotel in downtown Dallas.

We were very happy. I mean, Lamar and I had such a strong connection that we were married exactly thirty days after we met. We loved the idea of being husband and wife, and most of the marriage was really great.

Being in Dallas was challenging because I missed my family back in L.A. One day I decided that I needed to get out of the apartment and *do something*. That's when I came up with the idea of going to the gym.

I've never been the type of person who deals with her tough moments by sleeping or watching TV in the middle of the day. My brain doesn't work that way—I'm not that easily distracted—and I have a tendency to obsess and drive myself crazy over even the tiniest problem. So for me the solution is to keep really busy, to find a way *not* to obsess, and I usually do that by visiting with friends, going to see family or going to dinner or a show—anything that will occupy me. And really, how do people fill the hours in their day? They take care of their kids or hang out with family or go shopping. But in Dallas, I had none of those escape routes. I was completely isolated. And one morning I remember thinking, *Hey, I'm here at the W, in this nice apartment, and I don't know a single person I can invite to lunch. But there's a gym off the lobby.* All I had to do was get on the elevator, zip down five floors, and I'd be there. I knew they'd have TVs in the gym. I'm not good at *just* watching TV, but if I can do cardio and watch TV at the same time—that's a winning combo.

I felt alone with my thoughts and without direction, and it wasn't a good feeling. But once I got into my sweats and walked into the gym, I felt like I was a million miles away from my problems. And I realized that even though I was alone at the gym, I wasn't lonely. I didn't care that I was by myself. You're almost always by yourself in the gym. That's the point, right? To work on your self, your physical self. I was doing something constructive. And that felt pretty good.

The gym was clean and very luxurious, and there were only three or four people there. I got on an elliptical and turned on the TV and suddenly I was transported to another place, away from myself and my brooding thoughts. As soon as my heart started pumping, I was in a really good place.

That's how I began to deal with my own isolation—by visiting the hotel gym every day, sometimes twice a day. At first I was just going through the motions; I was lonely in our apartment, and I was motivated to get out. As the days turned into weeks, however, I began to look forward to the workouts. I loved sweating. I loved the feeling of accomplishment when it was over. And later, lying in bed, I loved the way my muscles ached. Exercising made me feel alive.

Beyond that, it energized me. After a good workout, I feel so full of adrenaline that I'm ready to do fifteen things at once, and I often have to slow myself down and get a grip. It's crazy—like I'm on speed or something—but crazy in a good way. The idea that an hour of exercise can have such a profound effect on my mood and on my energy levels is what keeps me going back for more. I mean, think about it: *Exercise gets me high!*

Of course, once you come back to earth, you still have to deal with daily life, and my life was far from perfect. This was the first time I had been away from my family, and it wasn't easy, but I made the most of our time together.

Christmastime away from my loved ones was especially hard. I missed those noisy Christmases in Los Angeles, surrounded by my loud, happy family, with wild children underfoot and good food and laughter and that wonderful sense of belonging.

I made the best of it, though. I got permission from the hotel manager to put a Christmas tree in our suite, and we decorated it together and that ritual made it feel like a real home. But it wasn't the same as being at home, of course. Every Christmas Eve my mom throws a huge party, and this was the first time in my life I was going to miss it. And that was hard, because the Kardashian Christmas Eve party was a family tradition that went back to before I was even born. Every year, in early October I'd begin to look forward to the party—who we'd invite, what we'd make, what I'd wear. Talking to my mom on the phone in the days before Christmas made it that much harder, but I realized I needed to be strong and make the most of my time with Lamar, and I knew there were plenty of other Christmases ahead of us.

Another tradition was for the entire family to wear matching pajamas and have our picture taken, and I was sad about missing that, too. But my mom sent us matching pajamas, the same ones she gave everyone else, and Lamar and I took our own picture in Dallas and shared it with the family.

When we went to bed that night, I pretended I was going to be waking up with my family, and when I got up, first thing, I called them. And you know what? It was fun. I was happy to be there with Lamar in our matching pajamas.

Still, it was a big emotional challenge—being away from my family for Christmas for the first time—and Lamar kept apologizing, but I told him not to worry, that *we* were a family now, and that everything was going to work out. Lamar missed them, too, though. When we were first married, my family welcomed him with open arms, and he never stopped expressing his gratitude. "Your family was one of the reasons I knew I wanted to marry you," he told me. "I love your family." Lamar is an only child, and his mother passed away when he was very young. Being so warmly embraced by us meant the world to him, and being away was hard for us both.

We couldn't even spend the day in bed together! The NBA lockout had been going on since July and the season actually began on Christmas Day.

We'd had a difficult couple months. Lamar and I had just dealt with a death in our family, then he was traded from the Lakers to the Mavericks very unexpectedly, which broke his heart yet again in such a short time span. By nature, I'm a people pleaser and it is draining both physically and mentally to please someone who is emotionally destroyed. There was a lot on my shoulders—five months in this isolated situation, doing battle with my own emotions but trying to be strong for us.

That's when the gym became a lifeline. It didn't make the pain go away, of course, but it made it more bearable. It made me realize that I was exercising more than muscles, and that the small but noticeable physical transformations that I was seeing were creating emotional transformations, too.

Being physical was in my blood, and exercising regularly made me think back to my childhood. I was always an active person. As a kid, I was into sports: soccer when I was really young, and basketball and volleyball in middle school and beyond. I liked basketball and volleyball best because I was tall and I was usually an asset to the team.

But I was always a little overweight, too. Whenever I was stressed or struggling with emotional issues, no matter how insignificant, I would turn to food.

When my parents got a divorce, for example, I would eat all the time. Our mother was constantly cooking for us, because that's what mothers do; they nurture their kids. Then Dad would swing by and pick us up and take us to McDonald's, because that's what fathers do. I guess this created a strange link between stress and food, which seems to be the case for many, many people, and as a result I would often turn to food for comfort.

Back in those days, people weren't as conscious about what they put into their bodies, so my parents didn't pay much attention, but that has certainly changed. Now, for example, my sister Kourtney doesn't let her children eat gluten, and she keeps them away from dairy, but twenty years ago, nobody ever gave much thought to either gluten or dairy.

On the other hand, both of my parents encouraged me to do sports, which might have been their way of keeping my weight from getting out of hand.

In addition, there was also the small issue of genetics. When I was very young—a preteen—I came to terms with the fact that I was always going to be curvy and bigger than most of the girls around me. I remember thinking, *This is who I am, a big-boned girl, and this is what my body's always going to be like.*

Once I hit puberty, though, I had a growth spurt, and I guess it made a big difference. I remember my mom's friends oohing and aahing over the change. "Oh my gosh, Khloé! You are so skinny!" I don't think they meant *skinny* skinny; I think they were basically noticing the change. And as they kept pointing out how good I looked, it made me wonder how I had looked *before*. Honestly, I had never thought of myself as chubby, and I certainly never thought about my weight. And this whole issue of food awareness is actually very new to me, something I've paid attention to only in the past couple of years.

In fact, I was so comfortable with my looks that in some ways they shaped my personality. I was a happy girl, cheerful and upbeat. I didn't think about my weight, and as a result I wasn't as stressed out as most other girls my age. People saw me as easygoing and lighthearted, and they were drawn to me; that was a nice side effect of not being weight conscious.

Years later I was still a joyful girl, and my natural buoyancy and exercise carried me through the early months of 2012. Then in April Lamar parted ways with the Mavericks, by mutual agreement, and we returned to Los Angeles.

I was super excited to be home. Los Angeles was my city. Everything was familiar, and it was nice to know that I could hop in my car and drive over to see my family and my friends whenever I wanted. I also like structure and routine, and being home, in familiar territory, made life much more manageable.

Of course, there was one big change: In Dallas, the paparazzi were few and far between. But in L.A., we couldn't get away from them, and it was oppressive. Even worse, if we were *not* smiling in a photograph they took, it fueled all sorts of rumors.

It was crazy. We were happy, and the press had no evidence to the contrary, but reporters were telling the world that our marriage was in trouble. Of course, a month later, the story they were telling had changed. With no evidence to support this either, the press began reporting that I was pregnant and that we were more in love than ever.

This constant imposition on my private life was exhausting. It actually got to a point where I was tempted to deal with the stress by sitting home, behind closed doors, and eating. But then I really thought about it, and my recent experience in Dallas, at the W, convinced me that there had to be a better way and that food wasn't the answer, so once again I began going to the gym.

Every time I left my house, the paparazzi followed. In cars, SUVs, and—from time to time—even helicopters. So I'd crank up the music and make the short drive to the Equinox in Woodland Hills. As soon as I parked, however, they were all over me, snapping pictures and shouting questions—"Is it true Lamar cheated on you?" "Is he doing drugs?" "Are you guys splitting up?"—and it was both painful and mortifying. I had heard all of the rumors, of course—they were on TV, on social media, and in the magazines—but the endless yelling was really unpleasant: I didn't need to hear that negative bullshit. Every day felt like an attack.

It was also humiliating; it got to the point that leaving my house would give me social anxiety. People would turn to see what all the fuss was about, and it got so I couldn't stop for gas or walk into a Starbucks without creating a scene. It was surreal. I had never been scrutinized to that degree. All of this was enough to make me paranoid, and I began to feel like I was being watched all the time (and maybe I was).

My solution was simple: I bought a pair of headphones and would slip them over my ears and crank up the music before I got out of the car. And it's funny, because when I look back at this period in my life there are hundreds of pictures of me with my headphones on, totally unfazed by the roving packs of paparazzi. I loved it. It's, like, "Hey, idiots—I literally can't hear you!" It was actually pretty funny.

The gym was a genuine oasis—a refuge and a sanctuary. No one bothered me. Not the paparazzi, who had to wait outside, and not the other clients. We were all there doing our own thing, and I enjoyed being around people, not locked up in my house. I didn't feel the need to talk to them, and they respectfully gave me my space, but I definitely found solace in being surrounded by humanity. (I also loved the sweating part!)

It's not selfish
to love yourself,
take care of
yourself, and
to make your
happiness
a priority. It's
necessary.

—Nancy Hale

How to Lose Ten Pounds in Ten Days—Not!

Within a few weeks I started losing a little weight. I had never thought, "Gee, I need to lose ten pounds in ten days," but the weight came off regardless, a little bit at a time. And I didn't weigh myself, either. I would walk into my closet, for example, and try on a skirt I hadn't worn in a while, and I would find myself astonished by how good it looked. A month earlier, that same skirt had been too tight; now I felt great and looked great. I don't think anyone should get fixated on numbers. For me, it's not about how much I weigh, but how I feel both mentally and physically. And of course about *how my clothes fit*.

Losing weight didn't change the situation at home, unfortunately. Some of the rumors were actually close to the truth; the marriage really was floundering, but my new self-possession definitely changed the way I handled it. I was stronger, physically and emotionally.

When the press wasn't writing about our relationship, they became obsessed with my workouts, and the angle was generally pretty much the same: *Khloé Kardashian—How She Lost 10 Pounds in 10 Days. Khloé Kardashian Wearing Waist-Training Corset. Khloé Kardashian Shares Her Surprising Secret to Weight Loss.* The media tends to take the tiniest kernel of truth and blow it up beyond all recognition. According to the press, I had gone from being the fat one to developing an unhealthy obsession with the gym. This was completely wrong.

My workouts were not about vanity; they were about relieving stress. I had so much going on emotionally, and I was disinclined to talk about it, even with my own family, so the workouts became a form of therapy. One of the pleasant side effects, of course, was that I lost weight and developed muscle tone and generally began to feel good and look good.

One thing people may not know about me is that I'm very passionate. When something upsets me, I feel it right away, and my immediate reaction is to pounce like a lioness. But at the gym I soon discovered that I could take a moment, curb my natural inclinations, and save my ferocity for my exercise. I feel a tremendous sense of relief as soon I walk through those doors. And after a few minutes of boxing or running on the treadmill, I can literally feel each brick of stress crumbling away.

I tend not to be as open as other members of my family. Despite my profession, which puts me on public display, I tend to be private when it comes to matters of the heart. I tend not to share many details about my life, especially if they concern other people. So if I'm having a problem at home—which I was, admittedly—I would keep it between the two of us. A marriage is about two people, not about your extended family, and I think those two people should try to figure it out themselves. And that's what I tried to do, and what I continue to do to this day.

When life frustrates me, as it frustrates us all, I turn to my sanctuary, the gym, the one place where I can be alone with my thoughts. The gym lets me work on my own problems and my own issues at my own pace, and so far it has been the best medicine I've found.

Alone with My Thoughts

The gym is also a place that is all about me, me without guilt, and that's a good thing, because I believe that everyone needs to carve out a little private time. In my case, with so much of my life lived in front of a camera (or being chased by cameras), I cherish whatever moments of quiet and solitude I can find. The gym gives me time to be alone with my thoughts, to try to get a little clarity in my own way and on my own time.

In the past, I have at times struggled with feeling that I've said too much, and sometimes people used the information against me. Not fun. If I'm in the gym, however, working it out with myself, that's not a concern. When I take that time for myself at the gym, I can play out all the different ways a conversation can go; I can think through the consequences of any action I might take; I can approach a problem calmly, rationally, and thoughtfully.

Besides, I don't want to dump my problems on the people around me, especially if I haven't had time to think about them, and I certainly don't want to share *only* when I'm in a crisis. On the other hand, most people do open up primarily when things are *bad*, when they have something to complain about. I guess that's human nature. Seldom do I hear them saying, "Oh my God! He showed up for our date with a dozen yellow roses and said he was really looking forward to getting to know me!" Usually I hear someone say something like, "You know what that asshole did to me last night?"

That's just the way we're wired, I guess. We'll call our best girl-friend and with great drama and anger tell her the *bad* thing our boyfriend has just done, not the good. So while it's perfectly normal to express the lows in life, I find it far more important, and far more pleasant, to speak of the highs.

Another downside to oversharing is that you get a lot of opin-ions, and most of those opinions are from people who don't really know the whole story (probably because you're not sharing all the details, and you're definitely not sharing the *good* ones). When you listen to too many opinions, you get confused and lose track of your

own voice. And that should never happen. Who are you going to listen to if not to yourself?

The thing is, every relationship is different, and when you start talking about your problems, other people tend to talk about theirs. Before you know it, you are making all sorts of crazy comparisons, like the time one of Kim's exes—my least favorite *ever*—started complaining about life at home. "Why don't you cook for me?" he told Kim. "Khloé cooks for Lamar all the time." This happened in front of me, and it really upset me. I told him, "That is so rude! How dare you compare our relationships? And why are you being so aggressive? The right thing to do is to ask Kim if she'd consider cooking for you from time to time."

He didn't treat Kim with respect; he wasn't kind, and, unfortunately, he didn't get my point, which I guess is one of the many reasons he is an ex.

As a person, you are unique. And your relationships with others—lovers, parents, and friends—are unique. No two relationships should ever be compared. Other people may look happy, but you don't know what's happening behind closed doors or what a smile might conceal. As human beings, we often look to others to gain insight or to learn something new. But that habit also makes us compare ourselves to others, and the dynamic in every relationship is different. It's great to be inspired by a happy couple. I'll see people interacting during a challenging moment, and I'll think, "I wish I could handle things as calmly and with as much maturity as they do." But does that really help me do a better job in my life? I think not. I can learn from my loved ones, but there's a limit. The reason why we struggle with insecurity is because we compare our behind-the-scenes to everyone's highlight reel. The fact is you will never know what happens behind closed doors, so making comparisons

to other people's lives is really only hurting you. If I am always comparing myself to others, I will forever be at war with myself. And who needs that? I like me just fine, thank you very much, flaws and all.

At the end of the day, we are all imperfect human beings. The journey is about growing and evolving and forever striving to become a better person. Bad things happen to us all; it is how we respond to those unfortunate events that defines the quality of our life and the lives of those around us.

As John Donne wrote, "No man is an island, entire of itself; every man is a piece of the continent, a part of the main." We need one another to find fulfillment in our lives. And to find fulfillment we need to reprogram ourselves to refuse to wallow in the negative and to celebrate the positive. We will manifest beautiful things this way. I'm all about manifesting the goodness in others and in myself.

You Can't Control the Outcome

As things got worse on the home front, I began to rely more and more on those sanity-saving workouts, and I tried to make more time for them. I was in my own little world, sweating away my personal problems and managing pretty well, but the situation at home took on a life of its own.

The thing is, you can't control other people, and you can't control the outcome of situations, and if you think you can, you will soon discover that you are badly mistaken. The other thing I couldn't control was the press, who were hungry for details and invariably got things wrong.

Unfortunately, Kim and Kourtney and the rest of my family

couldn't avoid the tabloids, and they all began to suspect that it was more than idle gossip. "We know something's happening, Khloé. Why don't you tell us about it? You're safe with us."

Finally, that's what I did—I told them. And I remember how blown away they were. Hurt, too, because I hadn't shared. So I explained myself. "I wanted to protect Lamar," I said. "I know how badly he wanted and needed this family. I didn't want people to judge him or blame him. And I didn't want him to feel like I was giving up on him."

At one point, I actually went to the producers and said I needed some time off from the show. One of them was very surprised. She had been with *KUWTK* (*Keeping Up With the Kardashians*) for eight years, and I had never, ever asked for any time off. She took me aside and asked me what was wrong. I told her, "Nothing. I just need some family time." But she knew. And many others on the set suspected. How could they not? But I needed the time. I was living 90 percent of my life in front of the cameras, but the other 10 percent was and is sacred.

Lamar and I went to see a couples therapist. And when I got into details about some of the problems we were having, she was a little surprised by the way I recounted the stories.

"You tell me these things in a very matter-of-fact way, with very little emotion," she said. "Most people would be hysterical in this same situation, but you describe it as if was happening to somebody else." And I said, "Yes, that's true. In the past, whenever I spoke about an emotional situation, I would get emotional and upset all over again, and I didn't like it. But lately I've been teaching myself not to do that. I want to be less emotional and more matter-of-fact. I guess I'm going for quietly analytical." She was really impressed. She said, "That's a real gift. It takes a big person to revisit tough moments without reliving the emotion. How do you manage it?"

And I said, "Cardio!"

My Trainer, Gunnar Peterson

After that moment in the therapist's office, I decided to work even harder on my own cardio-based therapy, and I went off to see Gunnar Peterson, who is affectionately known as the Trainer to the Stars.

I had met Gunnar when I was in my early teens, because my mother was one of his clients and she used to drag me to her training sessions. I won't name names, but every time I went to his gym I would run into major movie stars or major sports figures, and I guess that left an impression on me. Plus, my mother loved Gunnar, who over the years had become a close family friend, stopping by at Christmas and for birthdays, and generally becoming an honorary member of the family.

When I first went to Gunnar in 2012, I have to tell you that I was really intimidated. I was just beginning to get fit and I said to myself, "Okay, this is the real deal. This is exercise at a whole other level. I need to take this very seriously." It was weird. I didn't feel as if I had to impress Gunnar, but I did think I needed to show him that I was serious about getting into shape. And I honestly didn't know what to expect. I knew Gunnar a bit as a person, but this was Gunnar *the trainer*, and that changed everything. In fact it made me nervous. And it's funny because at one point I asked him, "Can I use the bathroom?" And he looked at me like I was a little crazy. Then he smiled and pointed me in the right direction.

Now I feel like I own the place.

Music to Sweat To

Beyoncé, "Love On Top"

Skrillex and Diplo, "Take Ü There"

Future, "Thought It Was a Drought"

Meek Mill, "Monster"

Rihanna, "Bitch Better Have My Money"

Nothing's perfect, but it's worth it
after fighting through my tears
Beyoncé, "Love On Top"

Beyoncé, "Drunk in Love (featuring Jay-Z)"

Rick Ross, "Sanctified (featuring Kanye West and Big Sean)"

Skrillex and Diplo, "Mind (featuring Kai)"

Rick Ross, "I'm Not a Star"

Nicki Minaj, "Truffle Butter (featuring Drake and Lil Wayne)"

Miguel, "Coffee"

Migos, "Handsome and Wealthy"

Migos, "Fight Night"

Meek Mill, "Tupac Back (featuring Rick Ross)"

Kanye West and Jay-Z, "Otis (featuring Otis Redding)"

Kendrick Lamar, "King Kunta"

John Legend, "All of Me (Tiësto's Birthday Treatment Remix)"

Jazmine Sullivan, "Dumb (featuring Meek Mill)"

Jadakiss, "Smoking Gun (featuring Jazmine Sullivan)"

Jay-Z, "Part II (On the Run) (featuring Beyoncé)"

Usher, "Confessions, Part II"

Skrillex and Diplo, "Where Are Ü Now (with Justin Bieber)"

I ain't gotta compete with a single soul

Nicki Minaj "Truffle Butter"

Kanye West, Big Sean, Pusha T, and 2 Chainz, "Mercy"

DJ Dizzy, "Rolling in the Deep (Adele Remix Tribute)"

Danity Kane, "Lemonade (featuring Tyga)"

Disclosure, "Bang That"

Beyoncé, "Crazy in Love (featuring Jay-Z)"

John Mayer, "XO"

Justin Bieber, "Change Me"

Hozier, "Take Me to Church"

Usher, "Twork It Out"

John Mayer, "Stop This Train"

A few months ago, my sister Kendall decided she wanted to train with Gunnar. She called me from the car on the way to the gym. "Can you please stay on the phone with me until I get inside?" she asked. I didn't question her. I knew she was intimidated because I'd been there myself. Looking back, I realize that dose of intimidation was useful. Sometimes that kind of fear is healthy. It means you're taking something seriously. And if you want to succeed at anything, you have to take it seriously.

By the time I began working with Gunnar, I already truly loved exercise, which was becoming a healthy addiction. I would exercise a few times a week. I started out with two sessions a week at Gunnar's. I would get there early and start out with some stretching exercises, and then I'd do thirty minutes on the elliptical. Sometimes I would jump rope, because I enjoy dancing around like a lunatic, and picking the right music is part of the fun. I'd listen to hip-hop and pop. I'm a big Beyoncé and Rihanna fan, and all of that top forty upbeat, happy stuff. The better the music, the harder I work out. If it's bad music, I fall completely off track.

The other thing I discovered at Gunnar's is that if I have a stressful day, my workouts are actually better. If I've had a good day, I'll still have a good workout, but it's missing that added component—frustration or anger or pressure—that adds fuel to the session. When I've had a bad day, I am more focused on working out, and by the time my workout is over, I've pretty much taken care of all of my aggression or frustration.

The other nice thing about working out consistently with a trainer is that you develop a relationship with him or her. Gunnar is almost like a therapist; I feel comfortable enough to share parts of my private life with him. So between the exercise and the talk therapy, I always leave the gym feeling great and ready to seize the day.

Of course it doesn't have to be a trainer. You can work out with a friend or a sister. It sometimes helps to have a workout buddy because you know she's waiting for you, and you can't skip out. And when you see someone regularly, there's an added benefit: You have someone to talk to, and talk can be therapeutic.

Some people do fine alone, of course, and I was perfectly fine with working out on my own during my Equinox days, but since then I've learned that I get more out of my workouts when I'm in good company. And if I'm truly alone, I bring my BlackBerry so I can type on those little upraised keys and communicate with my friends and feel connected to the larger world. I've even been known to *journal* on the elliptical, typing away on my BlackBerry, crazy as that sounds. I generally leave those sessions feeling as if I've totally cleared my head. It's like that great scene in *The First Wives Club*. Goldie Hawn plays a lush who drinks every night, but she has a great body because she trains in the morning to get the booze out of her system. After she's been on the treadmill for a while, her brain clears and she comes up with all sorts of kooky schemes for getting revenge on the ex-husbands. I know exactly how that works: not the revenge part, of course—that's never been me—but that post-workout clarity. You feel super sharp. You feel you can handle anything!

It's the best feeling ever. I will have days when I think, *I don't want to fucking drive to Beverly Hills today. I have too much to do. I'm tired. I'm cranky.* But I get there—you have to learn to push yourself—and I've never once said, "Oh, I really regret that workout!" I bet no one's ever said that. What human being is going to say, "I regretted working out today"? You regret *not* going, but you never regret getting through with it, even if you had to scream at yourself to get there.

If you think about it, a workout is not even 4 percent of your day. That's nothing! You can make time for that! If a cute boy calls you and says, "I want to see you tonight," you will somehow find the time to do it—even if you're shooting a movie or studying for your bar exam. So surely you can find time for the gym. It's all about wanting something badly enough and making that goal your priority. Many of us must learn to prioritize ourselves. We can get stuck in autopilot on an unhealthy schedule: get up, go to work, make dinner, go to sleep. But, it is up to us to make our health and our well-being part of our daily routines. If you truly want to grow stronger—in your body, but also in your mind and soul—nothing can stop you.

The other good thing about working out with Gunnar is that it gave me somewhere to go, an actual schedule, and I really needed that because by this time it was just me at home.

How Do You Fix a Broken Heart?

This might sound like a cliché, but when I fell for Lamar, I remember feeling truly complete. And with Lamar gone, I felt I was losing a part of myself. Fortunately, by that point, I already knew that ice cream and hibernation were not the answer, so I filled many of those extra hours by continuing to work on my physical and mental self.

Still, I'd be lying to you if I said it was a total cure. You don't just fix a broken heart. You need time. And it hurt, because I loved being married. I loved having a family. I loved waking up in the morning and having purpose. I loved Lamar's kids, too, and I tried to be a good stepmother to them. (I took some of my cues from my stepdad, Bruce, who had been an outstanding stepfather to me.) I reminded myself that I was a *stepmother*, not a mother, and that I wasn't there to take anyone's place in the children's hearts. As I'd learned from Bruce, my role was to be there for those beautiful children, to give them extra love, my own love, and not to compete with their mother for their affection. Bruce really had it down. He understood that his role was to be as present in our lives as we needed him to be, and he always was.

There were of course parenting lessons I'd learned from my own father, Robert Kardashian, and from some of the women he dated after he and my mother divorced. I'm not going to get catty here, but a few of those ladies had a tendency to be overbearing, and it wasn't very convincing, and others went in the opposite direction, shamelessly bad-mouthing my mother. I knew I never wanted to be that kind of stepmother. No child wants to hear negative stories about his or her parents. It was a valuable lesson, and it taught me that you can learn as much from bad examples as from good ones. When you marry someone, especially if they've had children with someone else, you need to be aware of what you're taking on. You've signed on for the whole package.

And the fact is, the more I bit my tongue, the easier it got. It reminded me of my workouts: I got stronger every day, and *not* reacting got easier and easier, especially on the days when I found time for the gym. In fact, learning to be a good stepmother was a form of exercise in and of itself. I started slow and got steadily better.

It reminded me of a friend who decided to lose weight. She began slowly, walking around the block every morning, and then one morning a month later, she called me. She had just run her first mile. She said she hadn't set any world records, but she didn't care: She felt an immense sense of accomplishment.

And the thing is, she had it right. You need to crawl before you can walk. When I first started working out, I took baby steps. I started with two workouts a week, maybe thirty-five or forty minutes each, and over time went more frequently and worked out for longer periods.

I used to be the queen of yo-yo dieting. My weight would fluctuate like crazy. It was really hard on me physically and psychologically. Lamar would tell me, "You can't get it back in a day." And he was so right. I used to beat myself up if I didn't stick to my routine, and when I got back to the gym, I'd do a two-hour workout to punish myself. This was really counterproductive because the next day I'd be so tired and sore that I would dread returning to the gym. When I finally understood that working out was for *life*, I was kinder to myself. I realized that I didn't have to rush or punish myself or overdo it, and that in fact slow and steady wins the race. Now I have no problem getting to the gym, and if I don't get there, I certainly don't beat myself up over it the next day.

Previous generations had a different approach to exercise—remember "No pain, no gain," "Feel the burn," and so forth?—and that is certainly a big part of my exercise routine. But if I had felt too much burning and too much pain when I was starting out, I wouldn't have persevered. Now I actually embrace those tired muscles. When my muscles hurt, my heart sings.

"What Do You Hope to Accomplish?"

By the time I started working out with Gunnar, I was doing a lot more than a mile, but my workouts lacked direction. So he sat me down and asked me what I hoped to accomplish.

Until then I didn't really have a goal. I just liked the way exercise made me feel. And it certainly wasn't about weight. I never thought I was fat. In fact, I always felt beautiful in my own skin. Of course, when my sisters and I started getting attention, people tended to refer to me as the fat Kardashian, or the ugly sister, and

I good-humoredly bought into it. "Okay, if you say I'm the fat one, I'm the fat one. I'm the fat funny one."

The fact is that I was kind of skinny at sixteen and didn't fill out till much later. But I was never one of those girls at the beach with the perfect bodies, lying around in a bikini with all the self-confidence in the world. I had self-confidence, too, but not in a bathing suit—not in a one-piece and certainly not in a bikini. And while I genuinely liked myself and felt pretty darn cute, I was self-aware enough to know that no one wanted to see me showing skin on the beach.

Being big or a few pounds over my "ideal" weight was not then and is not now an issue. In fact, because I believed I looked good—notwithstanding what everyone else thought—I always carried myself with confidence, and I learned long ago that people find confidence attractive. If you walk around thinking you're pretty cute, people are going to believe it. And I *believed* I was cute.

And sure, when people began to call me the fat one, I was curious about their perception. Sometimes I would look at myself in the mirror, trying to figure out what they saw and questioning my sanity, because I couldn't see myself the same way. Did I think I was fat? No, not really. I had always been a big girl, and I was still a big girl, but the weight didn't bother me. On the other hand, when I looked at old pictures of myself, trying to get a clue, I did notice that I looked unhealthy. My color and skin tone was off. That's when I realized that exercising was actually making me look healthier, undoubtedly because I *was* healthier. It actually gave me a bit of a glow.

I never thought about losing weight. I know it sounds strange, but to me, it wasn't about the scale. I really began paying attention to the pounds only after I started working out, when they began to melt away. Losing weight was a pleasant side effect, not the goal.

To me, exercise was about how I *felt* in both body and mind, not about my weight.

But many people *do* struggle with weight issues, and for them it *is* about losing pounds. Let me make a suggestion: Don't weigh yourself. I don't. I don't even have a scale in my house. If you weigh yourself every morning and you don't like the number on that scale, it's going to affect your mood. It might even ruin your day. That's why I'm against it. For me, it's all about how you *feel*. For example, the other day I was going through my closet and found a pair of jeans that I hadn't worn in more than a year. They had never been all that comfortable, but suddenly they fit. And I felt fabulous in them. I didn't need the scale to tell me how to feel; my jeans did. They felt great, and I couldn't ask for more than that.

Women also torture themselves over sizes. They go shopping and they can't fit into a size 4 and it makes them crazy. Well, I don't care. I could be a size 10, but if I look and feel good, that number is just as meaningless to me as the number on the scale.

I learned not to make myself crazy with numbers. It's counter-productive. I was exercising to stay sane, to keep going when I felt sad and helpless, and I wasn't about to ruin it by relying on mean-ingless numbers to measure the results.

And think about it—what a waste of endorphins! You do all that hard work in the gym, and your body rewards you by pouring yummy chemicals into your brain. Then you go home and weigh yourself and crash. It's not about the weight, ladies, and it's not about the calories, either. I'll be flipping through a magazine and it'll give you these crazy examples: *If you ride a bike for an hour, you'll burn 500 calories! If you walk for 45 minutes, you'll burn 300 calories!* That is so not accurate. The number of calories you burn depends on many factors: your weight, your height, the amount of energy

Success is not
the key to
happiness.
Happiness is
the key to
success.
If you love what
you are doing, you
will be successful.

—Albert Schweitzer

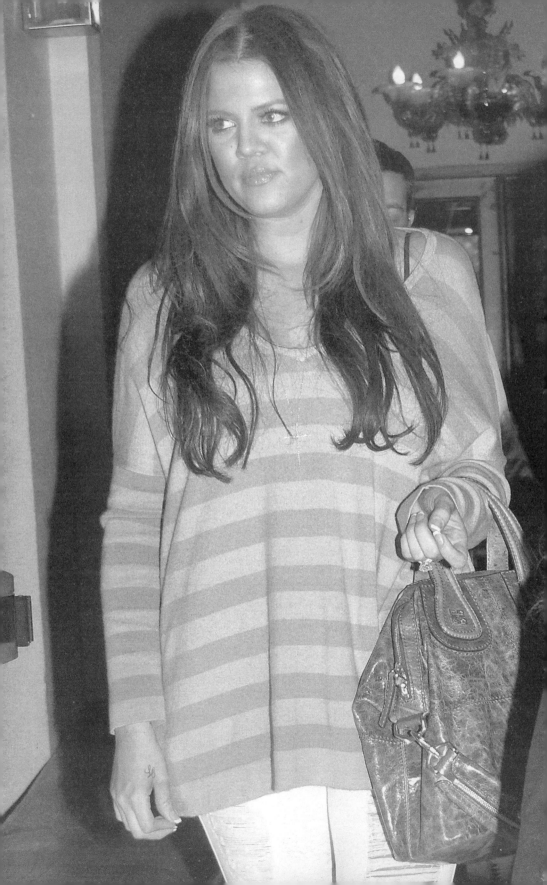

you're putting into that particular exercise. You don't have to count those calories. They mean nothing. The only thing that matters is how you *feel* or how you look in that little red skirt you haven't worn in three years.

Love What You Do, Do What You Love

If you want to know what really, truly matters when it comes to exercise, it's this: You have to find an exercise you can grow to love. If you don't, you won't stick with it, and nothing will change.

If bikes and treadmills aren't your thing, there are plenty of other options. If you don't enjoy what you are doing, you won't stick with it. I could never imagine running, for example. I hate it with a passion! But I love to box and jump rope. I like weight machines, too, but not everyone does. If you're not a fan, your body can be its own machine. You can do push-ups or planks. You can do jumping jacks. You can do stretches and squats. You can work your way toward your very first pull-up.

And you don't need a gym. Is there a pool nearby? Go swimming. Tennis courts? Take lessons. A mountain? Go for a hike.

When I was helping Kourt and Kim with their mothering duties, I would do squats while holding the babies! LOL! And that was hard, so I don't want to hear any excuses.

Plus look on Instagram. They have a number of very useful "no gym" workouts that can be tremendously motivating.

It really boils down to baby steps: one little step at a time. You walk a mile and add a second mile when you're ready. You do three push-ups and work your way up to ten. You swim an extra lap every day until you're churning through the water like an Olympic champion. Remember, the only person you need to be better than is the you of yesterday.

So yes, you need to push yourself a little. Getting started is usually a challenge, and the temptation is to give up or not do it at all. But once you see results—and you'll see them quickly—you'll keep going.

Your body needs and wants exercise. But you have to talk your mind into getting with the program.

And different bodies have different requirements. I have a friend who started with short walks around the block, determined to lose weight, and actually lost three pounds that first week! Now she doesn't have to think about weight because she's become a committed runner and it's a nonissue; she is in the best shape of her life, as lithe as a gazelle. Other friends work out twice a week and watch what they eat and are just fine. My friend Malika doesn't ever do any physical exercise and she has a perfect body, the bitch! But me, no. I need my five days. Exercise makes me happy. And I have scientific evidence to back this up: Dopamine is a neurotransmitter in the brain connected to feelings of pleasure and happiness, and exercise gets it flowing.

Set Realistic Goals

The other thing that really, truly matters when it comes to exercise is this: Set realistic goals. And even more important, be realistic about how you intend to get there. As Confucius put it, "When it is obvious that the goals cannot be reached, don't adjust the goals, adjust the action steps."

I recently learned that 25 percent of New Year's resolutions are broken in the first week, and that 80 percent of new gym members drop out within eight weeks. I think this is largely due to not having realistic goals. If you don't have something to shoot for, something *doable*, you are going to become easily discouraged. It's fine to aim for the moon, but remember that making change in your life is hard and you'll need to take baby steps on your way there. If you expect too much from yourself, you'll never get past the early disappointment.

I have a few suggestions on this point.

1. Write down your goals. If they're unreachable as stated, *re-write* your goals.

2. Start small. For example, *I will go to the gym Tuesdays and Thursdays after work.*

3. Devise a working plan. For example, *If I miss Thursday, I'll make it up on Saturday (but I won't overdo it).*

4. Reward yourself from time to time. Getting strong is *not* about self-torture.

5. Ask for help. If you don't know where to start, find someone who does. It often takes more courage to seek help than to act alone.

6. Praise yourself. Every time you go to the gym, pat yourself on the back. It's important to remind yourself that you are on the right path and doing great.

7. Be specific. A goal should have a time frame, but it needs to be realistic. If you want to fit into those jeans by summer, don't wait till late May to start working out.

Losing thirty pounds in thirty days, as is promised in many magazine articles, can be done, but only by some people. And if you happen to be one of those people, and you get there in thirty days, have you ever wondered what happens afterward? Well, I'll tell you: The pounds tend to come right back, and often in less than thirty days. You had a goal, you reached it, but now you want to take a little break from all the torture. And it *was* torture because your approach was all wrong.

For me, when I see books or read magazine articles that promise to transform your body in thirty or sixty days, I might flip through them, out of curiosity, but I already know that short-term formulas don't work. I have tried them all. I have tried every fad, followed every diet, believed every lose-weight-fast article. The one thing I can tell you for sure is that there are no quick fixes. The only lasting solution is a lifestyle change.

If you want to be healthy, if you want to get in shape, there is no easy fix. It's a lifetime commitment. But the irony is that this commitment can be the most pleasurable part of the rest of your life. There will be lapses, of course. None of us is perfect. But that's part of the journey. Every time I mess up, I get back on track with more drive and determination than ever. And it's because I don't expect perfection from myself. If I have an occasional slice of cake, well, I wanted it and I deserved it. And it's not a crime. But if I have a slice of cake *every day*, that's a problem, and it's my job to find the solution.

Forget the Quick Fix

In December 2013, I filed for divorce. At that point, I'd been working with Gunnar for almost two years, but kind of loosely. There

was a lot going on in my personal life and I hadn't truly dedicated myself to getting strong yet. At one point I managed to make it to the gym twice a week—I wrote that down as a realistic goal—but with the divorce looming, I upped it to three sessions. (I guess I needed more meds!) My life was full of noise and confusion, and I was experiencing an intense mix of love and anger, so I had to find a productive way of getting those emotions under control. And the gym did that for me. I felt both strong and mentally clear, and the good feelings that accompanied those regular workouts made me understand that I had to commit myself to this forever. I like to say, *It's not a lifestyle, it's a life.* Maybe if I had six-pack abs I'd write a book called *Get Shredded Like Me in Seven Days*, but I don't have six-pack abs and I don't believe in short-term fixes.

That's one of the things I love about Gunnar: he's not interested in the quick fix either. He wants to do it right. Gunnar is all about building bodies, and that's what we were doing. I would come in with a picture of Jennifer Lopez's abs and I'd say, "I want those abs," and for the next two months he'd make sure I put extra time into my abs. I remember walking into my bathroom one morning, seeing my stomach in the mirror, and doing a double take. "Hello, baby abs!" I said, admiring my midsection. "I can't wait to meet your other ab friends soon!"

Another time I arrived at the gym with a picture of Beyoncé's ass and told Gunnar, "I want that ass." And we worked on my ass. The Kardashian girls are a little obsessed with their asses, and I'm no exception. I remember telling Gunnar, "I have a really high butt, and I need to work on the bottom part, because I like it when a girl's butt is meaty." And he immediately replied, "No problem. We're going to do that."

He's very positive, Gunnar, but he's also very honest. He'll never say, "That's never going to happen." He'll say, "Okay, we can

Obstacles are those frightful things you see when you take your eyes off your goal.

—Henry Ford

definitely work on that, but there are certain anatomical differences between you and Beyoncé, so we're not going to create an exact duplicate. Still, I promise we will get as close as we can."

I respect and love that Gunnar comes from a place of yes. That positive attitude convinced me that my goals were reachable, and it all goes back to the idea of setting *achievable, realistic goals*. Gunnar had his own weight issues as a child, so he understands what it means to struggle and stay on track. He also knows that most of us have food issues because he's been there. (I mean, seriously, who doesn't love food?)

I also love that Gunnar takes the time to explain things to me, to get into the science behind his thinking. If I ask him, "What does this exercise do?" he'll tell me, "It develops this particular section of your glutes." He is endlessly patient, because I am endlessly curious, though it's obvious that most people are far more interested in results than they are in science.

While I do spend a lot of time on my butt, I also pay a lot of attention to my arms, which had been a source of terrible insecurity for me for a very long time. If you look at my arms today and look at a picture of them from a year ago, you'll think I've had an arm transplant. They used be soft and mushy, and whenever I gained even the tiniest bit of weight, it always went directly to my arms. And whenever I lost weight, my arms didn't always get with the program. They still aren't where I want them to be, but I am proud of the changes I've managed. And that's another thing to keep in mind. We can be our own worst critics. It is important to praise yourself for all the work you've put into your body. Giving yourself positive affirmations is a huge step in staying on track with your daily push to work out and get stronger. It would be easy for me to look at my arms and be discouraged because there's still a long way to go, but instead I'm proud of what I've accomplished.

Instead of being self-critical, I have become my own favorite cheerleader.

I was also insecure about my double chin. (Or should I say my *endless chins*?) It felt fleshy and soft, and I sometimes joked about getting jaw reconstruction surgery. I have always been a huge admirer of women with well-defined jawlines, and mine was hiding behind soft, excess fat. I began to wonder whether I even had a jawline. Then I noticed that exercise was actually beginning to redefine my face. With steady exercise, that extra flesh began to evaporate.

Visible changes like that really keep you going. But don't expect to see them for a while! Sometimes you begin to wonder what the heck is wrong with you. You pant and sweat and ache and absolutely nothing seems to change . . . but a month or so later, OMG! Finally you understand what all the hard work was about. You look good and you feel good and that's all the motivation you need to keep going. It has come to a point where I even get excited on my drive to Gunnar's gym. I've got the music cranked, I'm singing along, and I can't wait to start sweating. Crazy, right? But crazy *good*. I promise you. Sweating becomes an addiction, and when you finish a workout you feel such a sense of accomplishment that this becomes an addiction, too.

Routine and Structure

At one point early in 2014, I moved to the Hamptons to do a show with my sister, *Kourtney and Khloé Take the Hamptons*, and I got a little careless about both exercise and diet. I fell out of my routine. I should have made an out-of-town plan, with all sorts of contingencies, but I didn't and it soon showed. There are too many good restaurants in the Hamptons. Also, Kourtney was pregnant at the time, and it was almost as if I was gaining sympathy weight. Plus every night she would go through an entire box of Nilla wafers, and I started doing the same. I'm not blaming Kourtney. It was my own fault. I didn't have an ounce of self-control. And if I wanted to eat like a pregnant woman for the next three months, I wasn't going to beat myself up over it. I just went with it.

The weird part is that Kourtney was the pregnant one and I was gaining most of the weight. A few weeks into it, I was watching an episode of the show in which Kim took Kourtney aside and told her on camera that I'd gained a lot of weight and that she thought my ass looked huge. Thanks to the miracle of recorded television, I now knew exactly what my sister thought, and I wasn't mad at her. How could I be? She was right. Plus my ass was getting big in all the wrong ways.

I actually tried to get back in shape while we were still in the Hamptons, cutting back on those evil but amazing Nilla wafers and even making it to a few spin classes. But I missed the structure I had at home. It's one thing to go on a vacation for a week—you can always make time for a daily workout, and it's not the end of the world if you slack off for a few days—but it's hard to stay focused if you're gone for extended periods of time. That's what happened to me. I lost my way a bit. I realized that I need routine and structure, so I'm a big proponent of scheduling. I also find that it's harder to make excuses when you have a routine. You set a time every day, and you stick to it. It's easy to say, "Well, I'm working fifty hours a week, and I get home tired." Or "I'm a stay-at-home mom with three kids." But anyone can find thirty minutes in the day, thirty minutes of her very own, even if it means getting up an hour earlier. Excuses are easy to come by. Getting in shape takes work. If it's important to you, you will find a way. If not, you will find an excuse.

That said, if you can stay healthy without a set routine, more power to you. At the end of the day it all boils down to doing it, and you're going to have to find your own way.

When I returned to Los Angeles, I was about fifteen pounds heavier—the press couldn't stop pointing it out!—but I got back in the groove in a big way. I was more determined than ever not to let all my hard, pre-Hamptons work go to waste. I would find structure and routine again. I would get up early, have my morning cup of coffee, then get behind the wheel of my car and sing my way to Gunnar's gym.

Man, it was harder than I thought! I'd lost so much ground that those first few days were brutal. Within a week, however, I was feeling better. Within three weeks, I decided to up my routine to five days a week, and a few weeks after that, I was back in fighting shape.

Around this time, someone said, "Are you training for something?" And I said, "Yes, I am. I'm training for LIFE!"

There's a lesson here. Even if you screw up from time to time, you can always fight your way back. And it's not as hard as you think. Your muscles have memory; they remember.

But I can't stress this enough: The plan is for *life*. Stay steady and you never have to get ready! People who buy into a thirty-day plan or who kid themselves into thinking that they're going to lose fifty pounds by summer are setting themselves up for failure. You might get there, sure, but most people don't, and they give up. And even the ones who reach their goal often take a break that never ends, and before long they're back where they started. Stop looking at the numbers on the scale. This is about *health*, not numbers. And stop being in such a rush. There is no elevator to success; you have to take the stairs.

A dream doesn't become reality through magic; it takes sweat, determination, and hard work.

—Colin Powell

Getting Motivated

Some people find it's easier to get motivated if they work out with friends or family. Some months ago, shortly after Kourtney had her third baby, she asked me if we could work out together. I had my doubts—I think it's important to work out with people who are on your intensity level, and I didn't think she was there—but I was blown away by Kourtney's determination. She puts a lot of energy into her workout, and we have fun together.

Kim—not so much. She works out often, but we have different body types and need different things from our exercise. She's not as intense as I am in the gym and thinks I'm a *beast*, which I take as a compliment. And she's a little too ladylike. I sweat, she *perspires*. Big difference.

Finally, when it comes to exercise, you have to do it for you. When I started getting into shape, most of the media had opinions, and the general consensus was that it had been a "very long journey" for me. All I could think was "Screw all of you people!" None of them seemed to understand that it was *my* journey, and that I was doing it for me and nobody else.

And it will be a long journey, trust me. A lifelong journey with me at the controls.

If you are exercising to make someone else happy (a boyfriend, a husband, a critic, a relative), it's probably not going to work. But if you're doing it to make yourself happy, you'll succeed. Success is a choice. Choose to win! After all, who doesn't want to be happy? Especially when all it takes is a little sweat, dedication, and tenacity. That's what makes you strong.

As far as my own personal preferences, I always start and end

my workout with stretches. (I even stretch before I go to bed because I've read—and now I know from experience—that it helps
you sleep better.) I love jumping rope, as I said, which burns tons
of calories and does wonders for all parts of your body—legs, arms,
stomach, core. I do a minute on, a minute off, and within three
minutes I am pouring sweat, which I love, partly because it gives
me such a great sense of accomplishment. I always take a jump rope
along when I travel. It's light and easy to pack, and you can exercise

in your hotel room (at least until the people in the floor below call the front desk to complain, LOL!).

I love squats, and I love lunges. It's all about your legs, your hamstrings, and especially your booty.

Planks are awesome. Everyone needs to do planks. And you've got to hold your position even when your entire body is shaking from the effort, because that's how you know it's working.

I love weight machines—all of them—and I especially love to box. Boxing is a great stress reliever, but it also totally shreds your back and your arms and makes for an all-around great upper-body workout.

At the end of the day, though, if you ask me what my favorite part of my workout is, I can tell you in one word: sweating. It's like all the poisons and all the bad feelings are pouring out of your body. And it's funny, because I was in Australia recently and signed up for a Pilates class, and an hour later the class was over and I hadn't seen so much as a single drop of perspiration! All I could think was "How is this over? What a waste of an hour!"

I like sweating so much, in fact, that I've gotten into indoor cycling lately, partly because that bicycle makes me sweat like you wouldn't believe. Being soaked is a good thing, people!

I also find ways to stay active outside the gym. My mom has a trampoline at her house, for example, for the nieces and nephews, and I'm on there with them all the time. I'm also the one who is always pushing friends and family to play touch football or soccer or volleyball or whatever. And if I can't corral enough people for a game, I like to hike. I live in a neighborhood with lots of hills and nice places to walk, and now that Kim's pregnant again, she loves to join me. It's mellow and you're outdoors; since Kim isn't as deeply committed to sweating as I am, it is perfect for her.

I love to swim, too. At the end of the day, swimming is probably one of the best exercises you can do. If you don't believe me, look at a swimmer's body, male or female. Strength, tone, and beauty all wrapped up in one gorgeous package.

Five Simple Rules to Get You Started with Exercise

Start small. If you haven't exercised in a while, try a brisk walk around the block and build your stamina slowly. If you like hiking, the same advice goes: Start on the mellow hills and keep reaching for new heights.

Find something you enjoy. If you don't like lifting weights, stay away from them. If you don't like treadmills, find another way to get your cardio. I like jumping rope. I like the hula hoop. I like boxing. I like strength training. I like pelvic curls (great for both your stomach and back). I like heel beats (one of the best exercises for your butt). You won't stick with the program unless you're having at least a *little* fun. And mix it up! Varying your workouts keeps things interesting and exciting and helps you stay on track.

Challenge yourself. There's a point where having fun isn't going to be enough. You have to push yourself to get real results, and the more you push, the stronger you'll get. I didn't like crunches and leg lifts when I started out, but now I love them. I didn't like lunges, squats, push-ups, curls, shoulder presses, or high kicks, but I do now.

Repetition is key. Consistent exercise is transformational. And guess what? Sometimes it hurts. But that's when you know you're getting actual results. When it stops hurting, it's time to add another ten pounds to the weight machine, run that extra mile, or hike to the top of the next hill.

You're tougher than you think. The moment you feel like quitting is the right moment to keep going. Trust me, you are going to surprise yourself. There's a cardiovascular exercise I absolutely love called 10-20-30 training (or more accurately, 30-20-10, but that name doesn't have a sexy ring). It goes like this: If you're running or on the treadmill or on an elliptical/bike/rowing machine, you push yourself for 30 seconds, push even harder for the next 20 seconds, and in the final 10 seconds push so hard you think you are going to explode. This is one of the best interval workouts ever! Not only do you burn calories faster, but you build endurance, and, most important, you realize what you're capable of. You'll be surprised. The only inspiration you will need to keep going is *you*.

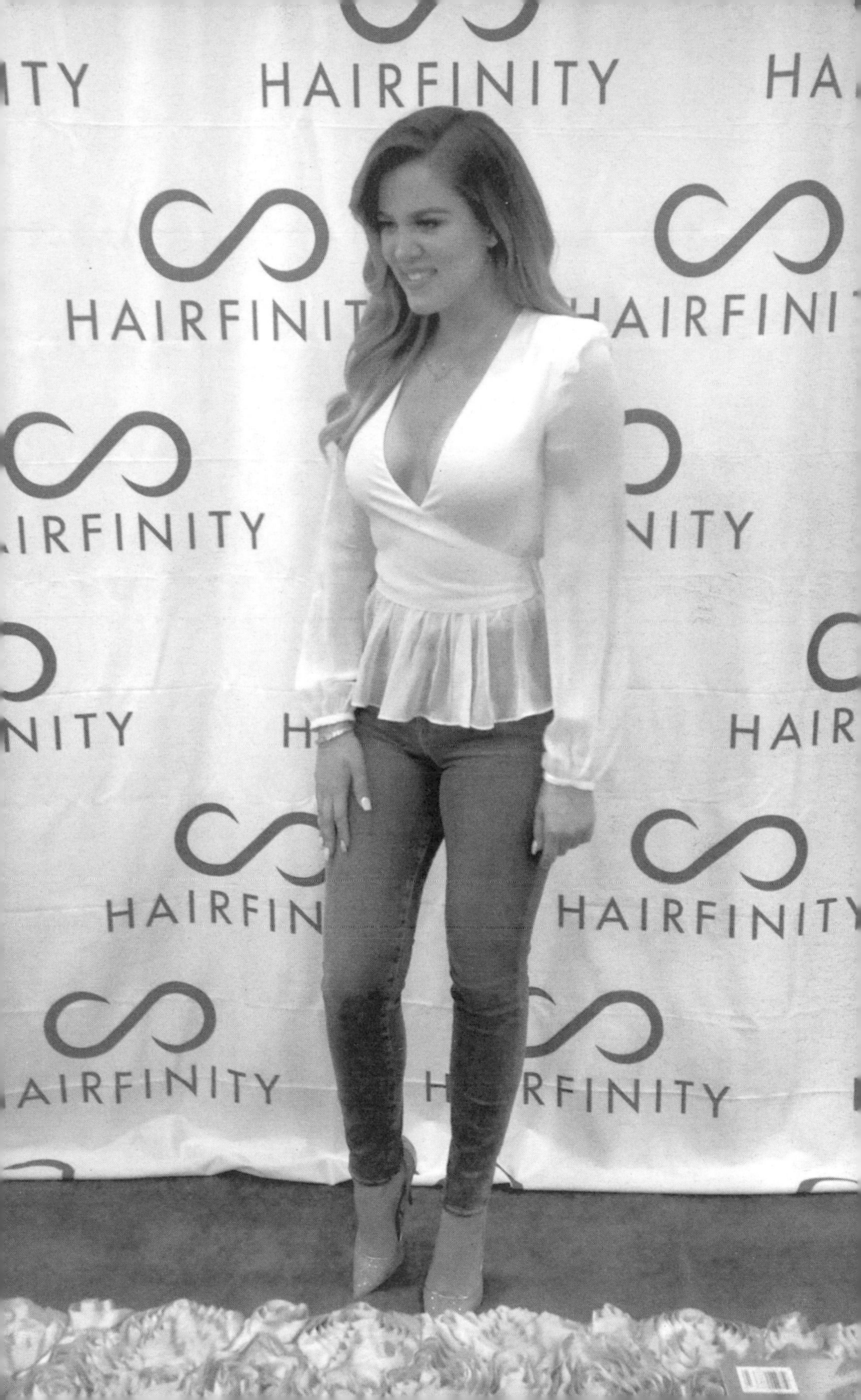
HAIRFINITY
HAIRFINITY

Gunnar Peterson

Author of *The Workout: Core Secrets
from Hollywood's #1 Trainer*

For most people, the single biggest challenge for getting into shape boils down to motivation. If you're not motivated, nothing good is going to happen.

And it's funny, because I often hear trainers talking about the way they motivate their clients, and I honestly don't get it. What do they tell them? "Hey, let's not forget to do our sit-ups tomorrow!" That doesn't mean much to anyone. If you're not motivated, you're not going to do your sit-ups. And if you are motivated, you don't need an outsider to remind you. *You are going to do them because you want to do them.*

That's pretty much what happened with Khloé. I had known her and other members of her family for many years—her mother is a longtime client of mine, as is her sister Kim—and Khloé decided she wanted to get serious about her body. When we talked about it, I told her that one of the most important elements I could provide was *consistency*: that my gym would serve as a little fortress, and that

I'm always there for her, holding down the fort. I do this for all of my clients. Los Angeles is a very transient city—*here today, gone tomorrow*—and many people are looking for a routine that truly anchors them. I try to provide this. When my clients are here, everything falls by the wayside—agents, deals, studios, friendships, marriages, etc.—and they can focus on getting strong.

But truth be told, this isn't just about my gym. I think any gym anywhere in the country can serve the same function. It's really about mind-set. If you make the commitment, if you go two, three, four times a week, the gym will eventually become part of your daily routine, maybe even the most enjoyable part. And if you're truly committed, you will eventually get to a place where you actually miss not getting your exercise, which is exactly what happened with Khloé.

When Khloé shows up at the gym, we have certain routines. We might work on her arms or on her abs, and I'm there to push her a little, but she seldom needs pushing. I'm there to structure the workout—the volume, the pace, the sequencing, and the movements. But I don't have to be a cheerleader because she's already motivated, already driven to be her absolute best, so mostly we talk about specific goals and about the routines that are going to get her there as quickly and as efficiently as possible (Or not. Sometimes the conversation isn't even exercise-related, which many clients find refreshing.) My job is to focus on results. It is also my job to create an environment where she can enjoy the journey. At my gym, the temperature is always right, I play music that works for the client, the machines are clean, and I'm there from 4:45 a.m. till nightfall—holding down the fort!

I'm not trying to downplay my role—if I wasn't useful, I wouldn't have clients—but I can't stress enough that you need to want this, and you need to want it badly. There is no other way to succeed.

As I said, though, you can create a similar situation for yourself at a local gym or health club or the Y (or in your garage or basement, for that matter). Develop a relationship with the staff or with one of the trainers. Sign up for classes. Get to know the other clients (if you enjoy the social aspect). The bottom line is, you need to find a place that works for you, and works so well that you are always eager to return.

So ask yourself what you need from a gym. Does it have to be open twenty-four hours a day? (Probably not. When was the last time you worked out at 4:00 a.m.?) Do you want to work with a trainer? Does it have to be a man? Does it have to be someone you can talk to? Should you take a group exercise class or would you be happier with a dance routine? (Maybe you want to do both.) It takes time to find the right program in the right environment, and in the process you're probably going to have to kiss a few frogs, but when you find your prince (or princess), you'll discover that it will have been well worth it.

The workout should be fun, but it should also be serious. Khloé and I have a good time, and we joke and laugh a lot, but it's also my job to keep her on track, to make sure she is always reaching to be the best possible version of herself. After all, at the end of the day, she's at the gym to get strong, to get into progressively better shape.

When Khloé told me about her book, she said she believed it was important for people to start slow and to find routines that they will enjoy, because otherwise they won't stick to them. I agree with her 100 percent. You don't have to love your workout, but you should choose a workout that you can *learn* to love. At some point, you should be enjoying it so much that you actually feel bad if you miss it. That may take a while, but if you stick with it long enough to see results, those results will provide the inspiration you need to keep you on track, and that's going to make all the difference.

Still, I have to go back to this issue of motivation. People tend to kid themselves, and I've heard more than my share of bullshit. "If I wasn't so busy . . ." "If I had more money . . ." "If there was a nice gym near my house . . ." These are just excuses, and the only victim is you. Khloé doesn't train with me because she has money; she trains with me because she is the kind of person who pushes herself, and she would push herself with or without my services. I know this to be true because she was an Equinox client long before she came to see me. And she's got the right attitude: *You've got to want it. If you don't want it, nobody can want it for you.*

Khloé is also smart enough to understand that becoming physically strong isn't about a short-term fix. *Lose thirty pounds in thirty days!* That's a loser's game, and I'm not talking about the pounds.

If you're in bad physical shape, that didn't happen in thirty days, and you won't be able to fix it in thirty days. You didn't get fat from one meal, and skipping one meal isn't going to get you back in shape.

The people who are selling you a short-term fix do not have your best interests at heart; they're in the game for themselves. That's life. Everybody's got a gimmick, everybody's got something to sell.

So be a smart consumer. Fitness, diet, health—everyone has a formula, and most of those formulas don't work. Thirty years of bad habits are not going to get reversed in thirty days. Use your head. You have one life, so why not make the commitment to live it right, and to live it *strong*?

When I first met Khloé, long before the TV show, I knew right away that she was as right as rain and very smart. Khloé understands that you have to work for everything in life: health, fitness, friendship, love, money. I don't know many people who understand that as clearly as she does, and I know even fewer who work as hard as she does.

Take that to the bank. And stop at the gym on your way back and get your workout in!

Chapter 2
Food

I was a mindless eater. I ate for comfort. I also ate out of boredom and habit. I ate when I was unhappy (which I'm sure many of you can relate to). I even ate chips because I love the crunchy sound they make. And I didn't give much thought to what I was eating, or what I was putting inside my body, except hummus, of course, which is one of my weaknesses.

Let me give you an example of mindless eating. When Lamar and I were still together and we were both in Los Angeles, I never missed any of his basketball games. There are eighty-two games in a regular season, not to mention the play-offs, and at least half of those were at home, and during that first year you'd find me at every single one, eating nachos. For the average sports fan, going to games is a treat, and the occasional nacho platter is not going to destroy them, but I'm doing this night after night—chowing down on nachos, chicken fingers, and assorted crap and more out of habit than hunger. The games would start at seven-thirty and seldom ended before ten, and sometimes Lamar and I would go out to dinner after, either alone or with friends. It was mindless eating.

I had no idea what I was doing to my body, night after night. It wasn't until I began to work out in earnest that I became aware of what I was eating. When I became more mindful about exercise, I became more mindful about eating. I was really conscious of wanting to put the right fuels into my body—to give me energy, to make me stronger—and part of it was that I was paying more attention to my health in general. I thought to myself, *This is the only body I have. Why am I treating it so badly? And what am I going to do about it?*

One of the things that I did about it was make an appointment to see Dr. Philip Goglia, a nutritionist. He is hysterical and I love him, and I totally connect with his energy. I also love the way he was able to break everything down for me. He had me provide a blood sample, which he analyzed, and the first thing he told me was that I needed to stay away from carbs. I was the type of person who was always going to have trouble with carbs. I sent my brother Rob to see Dr. Goglia as well, and Rob has the same issue. It's not that we couldn't have carbs, but that we have to avoid them after around four p.m. Apparently our bodies are not particularly good at breaking them down. And of course he told me to stay away from processed carbohydrates and stick to whole grains.

The other thing he told me to avoid was dairy, and I love cheese. Like many of my fellow Armenians, I was always chowing down on cheese cubes, so this was a huge challenge. But the moment I cut out dairy, limiting myself only to almond milk, I felt transformed. Within a week I had more energy than I'd had in months, and I was leaping out of bed in the morning, ready to seize the day. Phil explained that dairy tends to produce phlegm and mucus, which somehow clogs up the works.

The other unexpected side effect was that I lost thirteen pounds in less than three months, just by cutting out dairy. Though of course I was still exercising.

I was so taken with Phil that I told Kim and Kanye to go see him. They did that whole blood panel, too, and—wouldn't you know it?—Kim and Kanye are what he called *Ferrari body types*. Those two can process just about anything. Can you believe that? Life is so unfair!

At one point, I went on a hard-core diet for a week, at Phil's insistence, and within five days I lost 2 percent of my body fat. But dieting in that radical manner isn't natural or sustainable. I don't believe in short-term fixes, so I went back to regular dairy-free *mindful* eating. I think most diets are torture, which is why I don't believe in them. But, as is true with exercise, when you make a change and feel the benefits, you want to stick with it. And you know what else? If I want a piece of cake one night, I'll have my piece of cake!

The Cleanse from Hell

I know this from personal experience. Some years ago, when Beyoncé was doing *Dreamgirls*, she lost thirty pounds on a cleanse diet, and I decided to try it. It was one of the most miserable experiences of my life, absolutely horrible. I was so hungry that for days on end I was an evil bitch, and yes, I lost weight—for about a second. As soon as I abandoned that cleanse from hell, I gained the weight right back. That's the "quick fix": quick to go, quick to return.

I think some of those diets put your body into shock, and your mind follows shortly thereafter. I was *miserable*. And I get it: Sometimes you need a short-term fix, and you go for it. But my whole thing is about making changes for life. Yes, you have to cut certain things out, like soda or apple pie and ice cream, but you don't have to be a fanatic about it. If I go to the movies and want a Coke and some popcorn, I plunge right in. I don't believe in torturing myself. Then again, it's an *occasional* indulgence. I have a friend who has to have a Coke with every meal, and it shows on her body, so clearly she's addicted to the sugar. But if she could wean herself off the Coke—maybe limit herself to one or two cans a week—it would make a huge difference in her life, and the results might be enough to keep her on track.

To say, "I will never again have a piece of chocolate cake"—well, that's crazy. It's overwhelming. It feels so final. And it makes you want it that much more—the whole forbidden-fruit thing!

With that cleanse, for example, I started it just before my mother's birthday, and when the cake showed up, I almost died. You would have thought it was a box of diamonds! And it's funny, because I'm not that crazy about cake, but I felt so deprived that I almost wept with hunger.

The craziest thing is that I was convinced the cleanse was going to work. It was Beyoncé, for god's sake! My hero! She'd lost thirty pounds, so of course it had to work! But I was miserable. I'd been drinking lemonade and cayenne pepper for two days, my throat was burning, I felt like shit, and I had turned into a raging bitch. Long story short, I didn't make it through day 3.

As a result, I've gotten a lot smarter about fitness and weight loss, though I now know that not everyone sees it that way. I remember reading some blogs where people seemed fascinated by the fact that I had lost weight *over a period of months* instead of a month, as if somehow that were a bad thing. They didn't seem to understand that fitness is a lifelong journey. It's about trying to become a better version of yourself one step at a time. I'm not where I want to be yet, and I don't know if I ever will be, but I know that I am healthier and in better shape than I have ever been, and that I am really enjoying the journey.

Trust me on this: Slow and steady wins the race.

Water: The Magic Elixir

One day we're reading about the importance of water, that we need five liters a day, but a month later a contradictory story comes out saying we're all drinking way too much water and we should cut our intake in half. Phil was unwavering on this point: You need water, and you need a lot more than you think you do. Now, when I get up in the morning, even before my first cup of coffee, I drink a huge glass of water to get things started.

My little sister Kendall is a model and naturally skinny, and she wanted to be more muscular, so she started seeing Gunnar. When she complained that things weren't happening as fast as she hoped, I took her to see Phil. His advice? "Cut back on dairy and drink tons of water." And guess what? A few weeks later, I saw pictures of her on Instagram from the Met ball and her abs were insane. I immediately texted her, and she wrote back, "Thanks to Gunnar and Phil and their easy suggestions!" It was as easy as that. The exercise became way more effective because she cut out dairy and drank water. Of course let's be realistic here. Maybe she's got a *Lamborghini* body.

For a while, I was so into water I was even Instagramming about it. I wanted everyone to take it seriously, to drink, drink, drink. I even found ways to make water more fun. For example, I always keep a pitcher of water in my fridge, and I add mint, cucumber, and lemon. You just need a tiny bit. It's my own recipe for infused water, and I love it. Sometimes I'll just put a hunk of watermelon in the pitcher. Or if you want berry water, toss in a few strawberries or blackberries and let them sit for a while. It costs nothing, and it tastes yummy. I have five infusers—they are fairly cheap on Amazon—and I have five flavored waters in my fridge at all times. I like variety, and I love the way infused water tastes.

My sister Kim was over the other day, and she's pregnant again, and she tried the melon-flavored water and flipped. Now *her* fridge is full of flavored water!

The funny thing is, I used to keep iced tea and Snapple in my fridge, and I'd tell myself that they weren't unhealthy, but I'm no longer delusional. Occasionally I'll have an unsweetened iced tea, but the rest of those flavored sugary drinks are history. And fruit juices are a thing of the past, too. There are more than 100 calories in a single cup of orange juice, and there's nothing even remotely nutritious about that. When people have low blood sugar, others give them a glass of orange juice to quickly increase their blood sugar, so you have to ask yourself: Why would you want to increase your blood sugar when you don't need it? The obvious result is that an hour later you're going to totally crash.

Sugar is hiding everywhere. Sugar is 50 percent fructose and is immediately converted to fat. Little surprise we have an obesity epidemic. The World Health Organization says we should reduce our consumption of sugar by at least 50 percent. The American Heart Association suggests a maximum of six teaspoons of sugar per day for women, nine for men, and even less for children and toddlers. When you look at the numbers, you'll understand why fruit juices and soft drinks contribute more to obesity—especially in children—than just about anything else.

And I urge everyone to start reading labels. One can of Coke has forty grams of sugar, the equivalent of ten teaspoons. One glass of "healthy" orange juice has sixteen grams of sugar, or four tea-spoons, so it's not as healthy as you thought.

But water is magical. It's good for your skin and hair and nails. It helps you lose weight, it feeds your muscles, and it helps maintain healthy bodily functions. Some people think it's even a mood sta-bilizer, and I believe it, because I've seen the difference in me since I've been drinking adequate amounts of water. It's all about water. Flush, flush, flush. Go ahead, have some M&M's from time to time, live a little, but keep flushing.

If you want to take this one step further, there are some simple ways to detox. I love green tea, for example, and from time to time I will have nothing but green tea and water for an entire day. It really cleans out your system.

But you don't have to be that extreme. For example, that infused water I keep in my fridge is often enough of a flush, but you can make it interesting by playing with the ingredients. Try mixing pink grapefruit with a tangerine, a small orange, half a cucumber (sliced), and mint leaves. Or mix unsweetened cranberry juice and real cran-berries with water. Or try putting sliced apples and cinnamon sticks into your infuser. Refrigerate the infused water overnight and serve over ice cubes and you'll never go back to flavored drinks.

The old saying that knowledge is power is certainly true about your body, and especially about the way it reacts to food. When Kim went to see Phil, she listened very closely, followed Phil's advice, and lost a ton of weight almost effortlessly. Even if you have a Ferrari body type, the more you know about your engine, the better you can tune it.

And here's the thing: I love Phil Goglia, and I'm lucky I can afford to spend money on diet-related blood work, but your own body has the answers you need.

You can try cutting out dairy for a week. You can eliminate carbs the next week. You can eat less protein on the third week or eat mainly protein on the week after that. Your body will know within a week how it feels about these unexpected changes. In a way, you become your own laboratory. Your body's response will tell you exactly what it's going to take to run smoothly and feel right.

This goes back to setting realistic goals. As with exercise, you might want to jot down some goals for the week. *I'm going to eat less sugar this week*, for example. And again, baby steps—one restriction at a time. After a week, try something else—*no more white bread*—and so on, moving steadily forward. Keep doing this and it will become *a way of life.* I know your journey because it has been my own.

In terms of general advice, I know for a fact that dairy isn't very good for you. (I'm sure the National Dairy Council is going to hate me for this, but I believe it to be true for most people, and I know it's true for me.) I know carbs are rough on many people, because they tend to make your insulin levels spike, which can create mood swings, and beyond that, because carbs are hard to process. I don't think too much red meat is good for you, but I know plenty of devoted carnivores, and most of them seem happy and healthy, so I could be wrong. Maybe that whole Paleo-caveman thing works for them. And sugar, well—everyone knows sugar is trouble, but it's also yummy, so the occasional dish of chocolate soufflé isn't going to kill you.

Sometimes it seems like all the things that aren't good for you are the best-tasting! But again, make your own choices—you shouldn't suffer (or suffer too much, anyway). One size does not fit all! I have tried almost anything and everything when it comes to dieting. I had to figure out what worked for me and my body type. I also don't believe in depriving yourself. M&M's and cake and ice cream exist for a reason. Life is short. Enjoy it. But if your body isn't going to feel and look good, you're not going to be happy, so make a few *intelligent sacrifices*. It's worth it. As soon as you start making healthy eating choices, you will feel better, and sticking to the plan will be that much easier. In fact, you'll want to stick to it. I used to wolf down a piece of cake and feel comforted; now that same piece of cake (usually) makes me feel like shit.

Like I said, your body won't lie. Experiment. Listen to your body. The answers are inside you.

Dr. Philip Goglia

Nutritionist
Performance Fitness Concepts

One of the most important things I do with my clients is to teach them the difference between the foods that cause inflammation and the foods that don't. Ultimately the foods that promote inflammation will promote fat hoarding, and they will also age you more rapidly. I work with a lot of elite athletes, who are of course concerned about performance, and all of them stay away from inflammatory foods, but the health benefits apply to everyone. Which are the inflammatory foods? Yeast, mold, refined sugars, gluten, and ultimately alcohol.

When we say stay away from yeast, mold, refined sugars, and gluten, we're really telling you to stay away from carbohydrates—bread, muffins, bagels, and basically almost any of those fluffy baked goods. But if you're still determined to consume carbs, and there's no need to be afraid of them, go for the good ones: potatoes, rice, yams, oatmeal, oat flakes, oat puffs. They are rich in fiber, and some of them are filled with vitamins and minerals.

If you really want a sandwich, use one of those soft spinach-based or tomato-based burrito-style wraps, or even a pita, which is a low-yeast unleavened bread. It has one ingredient, and that's what you want.

Carbs are actually a good source of energy, and we all need them, but there is no reason to consume them at night. At night, stick to protein and vegetables, nothing else. Protein is meat with eyes: chicken, fish, steak, turkey. Eggs are a good source of protein, too. Fish is especially good at night because the fatty acids help reduce inflammation while you sleep. Nuts are good, too, but that's another category. (They have a higher fat-to-protein ratio than meat or fish and are a good energy source.) But absolutely no carbs at night. You don't want energy at night—after all, you're not going to be running a marathon—you want sleep. And when you're in deep sleep, you burn even more fat.

And vegetables are great. They promote digestion. You can't have too many vegetables.

Now we get to the question of alcohol. Like carbs, alcohol can be multi-ingredient or single-ingredient. Single-ingredient alcohols include vodka or tequila, which are made from potato, rye, grain, or agave. These are distilled, and the sugars have been removed. Wine and beer, on the other hand, are multi-ingredient alcohols, and they contain yeast, mold, and gluten. If you can stay away from them, great. If not, the rule of thumb is to drink three glasses of water for every glass of wine or beer to disperse the sugar and mold.

The other big inflammatory item in food is dairy. We always say dairy is like eating moderately hard phlegm, and when we describe it that way to our clients, it totally grosses them out. We say, "Look, dairy is for babies. We're the only animals in the entire animal kingdom that ingest dairy after babyhood. No one else does it but us." If you're asthmatic, you don't consume dairy—or you *shouldn't*, anyway. It inhibits oxygen utilization. It's highly inflammatory. It elevates triglyceride levels. There's nothing in dairy that's beneficial. If you lined up twenty of the best athletes in the world and said, "Hey, I came here to take your dairy order," guess what would happen? You wouldn't get a single order because any athlete that's concerned about performance, oxygen utilization, and digestion isn't going to go anywhere near dairy. It's especially bad for digestion. Irritable bowel syndrome, GERD (gastroesophageal reflux disease)—these have a direct relationship with dairy. As soon as we eliminate dairy from our patients' diets, those ailments disappear.

The one thing that really helps manage inflammation, the one truly magical element, is water. The general rule for water consumption is half an ounce of water for one pound of body weight, but many athletes will consume twice that amount.

The purpose of water—and the definition of water is that *fish must be able to swim in it*—is to regulate your temperature. If your water is low, your body can't effectively regulate your temperature, and it perceives that as trauma. At that point your body will start to hoard fat underneath your skin to act as a form of insulation and to help control your temperature, and this is not what you want. That's why water is so critical, because water really runs the show. I know people who have lost five or six pounds in a week simply by drinking more water. It not only controls you temperature but improves your digestion and helps get the toxins out of your system.

You have to teach yourself to drink water even when you're not thirsty. Start every morning with a big glass of water, and you'll feel the difference in a matter of days. Water releases fat as an energy source, so when you're properly hydrated you don't need fat to control your body temperature. Water thus helps you lose weight.

If you want to get into shape, good, healthy food is as important, if not more important, than exercise. And if you get hungry between meals, it's okay to snack, but keep it healthy. Fruit is good. So are nut butters, especially almond butter, but in reasonable amounts: A tablespoon should do you.

I don't believe in diets. I believe in eating right. If you want to be healthy, treat your body well and it will reward you in ways you never imagined. Make the commitment. It's the only body you've got.

Of course, when you find out what your body responds to, don't go crazy. It's not good to be a zealot about exercise, about food, or about anything else. And with food this becomes very dangerous: The things you force yourself to avoid become that much more attractive—that whole forbidden-fruit thing again. Honestly, don't get too extreme because that's the road to failure. If exercise is torture, you won't do it. And dieting is fine, but strict, overzealous dieting is also a form of torture, and at some point you're going to break down and get in your car and race to the grocery store for a pint (or two) of Tahitian vanilla ice cream.

If there's something in your fridge you can't resist, get rid of it. It stands to reason that you have to make a trip to the grocery store in the middle of the night for a certain snack, there's a good chance you won't do it. I'm obsessed with cheese, so there's no cheese in my fridge because I know myself, and I can see myself standing in front of the open fridge, chowing down. On the other hand, my house has plenty of giant cookie jars full of treats for my nieces and nephews, and I'm not at all tempted by cookies, so they can stay. So it's actually very simple: Don't keep something you really can't resist around. And don't pull that old trick where you stash the chocolate truffles out of sight on the top shelf of your pantry, just so you can pretend they aren't there, because you know they are and pretty soon they're going to be calling your name.

I know this from personal experience, LOL. Cut the cord!

Are You Really Truly Hungry?

Another food-related issue, and it's a big one, is hunger. Food and hunger are very closely related, of course, but most of us tend to eat when we're not hungry, and to keep eating long after we've had our fill.

We may think there is willpower involved, but more likely . . . change is due to want power. Wanting the new addiction more than the old one. Wanting the new me in preference to the person I am now.

—George A. Sheehan

I love pita chips and hummus. This combination is a guilty pleasure for me. I love the taste and the crunch. I could sit on the couch in front of the TV for hours, inhaling and enjoying that lovely crunch, and I've been known to do so, *often*. Just now, thinking about pita chips and hummus, I get hungry. And this is not even real hunger; it's about the comfort of the crunch. I love food with texture. Food that talks back! I love sushi, but it has to be on crispy rice. I guess I love *hearing* my food. Crazy, huh?

I used to eat in bed, too, but I stopped. I would lie there mindlessly eating like a hungry princess, and I felt so regal I wouldn't stop. Now I try to limit myself; what was once a habit has become an occasional treat. Mostly I eat at a table, my kitchen counter, or a restaurant.

Did you know that certain colors may influence your appetite? For example, a red plate is said to increase your appetite, while darker-colored plates might actually help suppress it. The color of your kitchen might influence your eating, too. Insane, right? Red, orange, and yellow are said to stimulate the appetite, so paint those walls. (Ever notice the bright colors at your favorite eatery? Guess why?) Try the cool colors—white, baby blue, mint green. You're not going to see any of those colors in a fast-food place because those crafty people have done their research and want you to eat more!

And I try to eat slowly. This is a BIG one because my mother is a very fast eater, and I learned to eat fast from her. But I taught myself to slow down, to really taste what I was eating. We don't realize how fast we tend to eat, and in situations that make us hurry—in the car, between errands, during a work break. Take your time with food; nourish yourself with love. It makes the experience so much more pleasurable, and you end up eating less.

Another advantage is that you know when you've had enough

and you stop. If you're sitting there gorging, you'll still be chowing down long after you're full, and you end up paying the price. How many times have you lain in bed after a huge meal, moaning and berating yourself for overeating? Well, join the club.

And while we're on the subject, restaurants are particularly dangerous. You sit down and the bread is calling to you, along with the olive oil. Then the salsa and chips arrive, with a big side of guacamole. Or the chef sends over a complimentary goat cheese concoction that's impossible to resist. So you dig in. And the moment you hit the wine, all bets are off. It's as if the wine is saying, "Loosen up. Have fun. Eat whatever you want—you deserve it."

And don't get me started on that whole low-fat craze! People were so excited about nonfat yogurts and fat-free chips and whatnot that when they first hit the market everyone got caught up in the revolution. As a result, people ate less fat but more carbs, and the carbs, particularly those with sugar and high-fructose corn syrup, were super fattening. Later, however, science began to figure out that fat wasn't really all that bad for you. In fact, the fat in your food is helpful because it tells your body when you've had enough. With low-fat meals, this didn't happen, and people found themselves eating far more low-fat food just to feel sated. It totally defeated the purpose. Plus the low-fat stuff didn't taste as good. So what do I do? I eat the good stuff, but I eat less of it, both because I know I need less and because I've become a more conscious eater.

Be especially careful about those low-fat options when you're eating at restaurants. Many chains have jumped on the low-carb bandwagon, but low-carb doesn't mean low-cal. Low-carb meals are often packed with fat.

The other restaurant problem is ordering. When you arrive, you're hungry, or you're supposed to be hungry, and everything on the menu looks good. So you order too much, and by the time your main course arrives, you're full. But since it's already in front of you, looking pretty, with your name on it, you don't want to be rude. So you eat it. And you keep eating until it's gone.

The message: Order less, always. If you're still hungry, you can steal from the plates of other people in your party.

It really boils down to three simple options. One, don't eat all the bread and junk they put on the table, even if you're hungry, and even if everyone else is digging in. Two, don't order an appetizer. At most, agree to share an appetizer with someone else, but make sure they put the plate in front of the other person. And three, don't feel obligated to finish your main course. In fact, there's usually enough in any restaurant meal for at least two portions. Make a conscious effort to divide it into two before you start and take the leftover half home for lunch the next day.

Not that complicated, right? Order less. Slow down. Be mindful. You'll eat less and enjoy it more. I know I do. My nacho days are behind me. I am serious about this one. It has made a huge difference in my life.

Clean Food, Healthy Body

This brings me to another issue, which I find totally fascinating. I read somewhere that people in Europe tend to be much more interested in food than most of us here in America, but that somehow they have far less of a problem with obesity and poor health. This sounds like a contradiction, but it makes perfect sense. If you care about what you eat, you tend to eat more carefully.

When I was in Paris for Kim and Kanye's wedding, for example, we never stopped celebrating, and in fact it felt like we were

eating around the clock. But I didn't gain a single pound. Later, looking back, I realized that in the course of the entire trip I didn't eat any processed foods. I found out that just about everything we were served was organic or had come from local farms, and it made a huge difference. The food tasted cleaner because it *was* cleaner, and it really got me thinking about this whole slow-food, farm-to-table business.

Unfortunately, here in America we're mostly about speed and efficiency; everything is go-go-go. That's why chickens in this country reach maturity in a week, with a little help from steroids, why cows get antibiotics, and why most farmers still spray their crops. But none of that stuff is good for us, and we need to start becoming more aware of what we're putting into our bodies.

Now, admittedly, if you start paying more attention to your food, you're going to find that you pay more for the good stuff. Free-range chickens are more expensive to raise. Ditto with grass-fed beef. Ditto with organic fruits and vegetables. But they are definitely worth the extra money, and because the food is richer and denser, you're going to find that you will eat less.

Farmers' markets are also good places to find healthy food. Here again, of course, you're going to pay a little more, but it's really worth it. Farmers' markets are about good local food, and that beats most of the stuff at your local supermarket. On the other hand, many of the big chains are beginning to get into organics, and competition might actually bring the prices down.

Being mindful when you're shopping for food is definitely the way to go. There are a lot of things in life that are beyond our control, but choosing healthy food isn't one of them.

The food you buy at the farmers' market is seasonal. It is fresh and delicious and reflects the truest flavors. Shopping and cooking

We can use decision-making to choose the habits we want to form, use willpower to get the habit started, then—and this is the best part—we can allow the extraordinary power of habit to take over. At that point, we're free from the need to decide and the need to use willpower.

—Gretchen Rubin

from farmer's markets helps you reconnect with the cycle of the seasons. As you look forward to squash in spring, savor sweet corn in summer, and bake sweet potatoes in autumn, you reconnect with the earth, the weather, and the turning of the year.

Did you know that food in the United States travels an average of 1,500 miles to get to your plate? All that shipping uses up lots of nonrenewable resources (especially fossil fuels), contributes to pollution, and creates tons of trash with all that extra packaging. Instead of polluting the environment, let's pay a little more at the famers' market and reap the rewards: healthier bodies, cleaner air.

When I started becoming more conscious about food, I used to keep freshly chopped fruit in the fridge. I'd buy it at my local supermarket, and I loved the fact that it stayed fresh for days. Then one night Kourtney came over and looked in my fridge and saw the fruit, which had been there for several days. "Do you know why that fruit looks fresh?" she asked, then answered her own question: "Because at the supermarket, they cut it up and immediately put preservatives on it." I couldn't believe it! I had never thought of that. But she was right. If you buy an apple at the farmers' market, it'll start turning brown shortly after you cut it. That's a good apple. It's real and untreated. But if your sliced apples and tomatoes stay fresh for days on end, you know they've been treated, and you should start shopping elsewhere. As a result of that exchange with Kourtney, I now buy my fruit whole and cut it up myself. And I get *all* my vegetables at the famers' market. Small price to pay for good health. Taking a shortcut—buying a quart of precut fruit at the supermarket—was damaging to my health. And seriously, how much energy does it take to slice your own fricking apple? Knowledge is power, people.

The Joy of Cooking

As I became more interested in food and good nutrition, I began to cook more. Sundays are a big cooking day for me, and I always have friends and family over, but I have to admit that I don't always cook the healthiest food. People love my breaded chicken, so I make that. And I eat it, too. (I told you: Don't be a zealot.) To balance things out, I always make nice salads and tons of fresh vegetables, so my guests have plenty of choices. Nobody leaves my house hungry. And if they think breaded chicken is the enemy, they have plenty of other options. But for me there's a clear distinction: Food isn't the enemy, as many women maintain; *bad* food is the enemy.

A couple of summers ago, the family decided it would be fun to take a cooking class together, and we signed up for a course at the Four Seasons in Westlake Village. We all went—Kim, Kourtney, my mom, even Bruce. It was a phenomenal class, focused mostly on basic, healthy cooking, and we all learned a lot—notably that home cooking should be about simplicity. If you want pheasant under glass, try a snooty restaurant.

I'm really happy I went. Since then, I've become a committed cook, and I am always looking for opportunities to learn new recipes. For example, if I go to a friend's house and enjoy the meal, I ask him or her to come over and teach me how to make it. I ask for a list of exactly what I need to buy and have the ingredients ready and waiting.

If you find cooking challenging, the best way to take the mystery out of it is to figure out how it's done. You can learn to make meals that taste good and are good for you. You'll also learn to make meals that taste great and are *not* so good for you, but that's fine, too. And you don't have to go to the Four Seasons to learn. They have cooking classes at your local Y or community center. If you go online, you can find reasonably priced cooking classes just about anywhere. Or you can learn at absolutely no cost: You'll be amazed at how many people post YouTube videos in which they walk you step by step through their favorite recipes.

The other thing about cooking is that it's very therapeutic. I like shopping for the right food. I like coming home with the raw ingredients and *creating* a meal. And now that I cook, my friends are always calling or texting: "You cooking tonight?"

My little sister Kylie texts me four times a week! "Do you want to cook for me tonight?" Yes, Kylie, I live to cook for you! But seriously, I love having her over. One day my mother told me, "You need to cook dinner for your little sisters once in a while, and I'm not talking about boiling pasta." I realized she was right. I started inviting Kylie and Kendall over and it has become a regular thing. Sometimes they even show up early to help me make meals and to figure out how to do it in their own homes. I love having people in my kitchen. And if you don't have a lot of family nearby, invite friends. Trust me, if you tell your friends you're cooking, they'll come right over. Even if the food isn't a resounding success, they will appreciate the company. I always find that the best times are around meals, especially the ones I prepare myself. This is a great thing to do with friends. Let's have a cooking party! Or "Hey, come over, spend time with me, and we'll make this special dish." It's super fun and active, and there's real joy and beauty in cooking.

Lately I've been getting lots of calls from Kylie. "Okay, that turkey burger, how does it work?" Well, I explain, you go to the butcher and get healthy turkey and they grind it for you. "What about that yummy tomato sauce? Where do you buy that?" You don't, I tell her.

You buy organic tomatoes and fresh garlic and you make it yourself.

Cooking is really magical, and I was surprised to learn that most of the women I know are pretty clueless about cooking. Everyone gets takeout, which is fine from time to time, but it's also a little sad. What happened to cooking for your family? I don't mean to sound dramatic or old-fashioned, but basic cooking isn't really that complicated, and I wish people put more time and energy into feeding their families. My sister Kourtney is the only one in my family who does that. For her, it's all about nurturing, all about family. And now that I am health-conscious, I totally get it.

If there's one final thing I want to say about food, it's this: Don't diet. When you diet, you are basically setting yourself up for failure. I mean, the word *die* is in there! You're not allowing yourself to enjoy the food you love, and it will only make you want it that much more. Make smart lifestyle changes, one baby step at a time.

Trust me: If you are mindful about your eating and you make healthy choices, the weight will disappear.

Once you get into the habit, it is easy to make healthy food choices. Of course, there are certain things I don't like. Green drinks, for example. They do absolutely nothing for me, beginning with the way they look. But that's just one woman's opinion, and I hear some of those concoctions are unbelievably good for you, so don't let me stop you.

Many people start their days with a health drink, green or otherwise, which is absolutely fine, but I prefer steel-cut oatmeal with flaxseed powder. I like it hot, with either water or almond milk, depending on my mood, though I know a lot of people think it's boring. I'll also have egg whites from time to time, another healthy choice, but seldom more than once or twice a week. There are endless and delicious ideas for nourishing, healthful food.

My Day on a Plate

5:00 a.m. I'm up bright and early and have a huge glass of water and a black coffee.

6:00 a.m. I'm off to the gym, ready to sweat.

8:00 a.m. Breakfast is another big glass of water, my Ideal Oatmeal, and a protein shake.

11:00 a.m. I snack on an apple with peanut butter or fruit and nuts.

1:00 p.m. Lunch is Chinese Chicken Salad.

3:00 p.m. Snack time! Homemade Hummus, chopped veggies, edamame, and another big glass of water (this time infused with fruit).

7:00 p.m. Time for dinner. I usually keep it pretty clean, and my favorite go-to is Steamed Veggies and Fish served with my Magic Mash-Up, and a glass of water of course!

9:00 p.m. I end my day with a bowl of fruit with plain Greek yogurt.

Cooking with Khloé
Breakfast with Khloé

Ideal Oatmeal
Serves 4

I love my oatmeal steaming hot. I always add a few tablespoons of flax-seed powder for an extra blast of nutrition in the morning. For a little variety I'll sometimes add fresh fruit—blueberries, strawberries, or raspberries—or chopped almonds and one or two of my favorite spices, like cinnamon, nutmeg, or cardamom.

    3 cups water or almond milk
    ¼ teaspoon salt
    1 cup steel-cut oats (I recommend Bob's Red Mill Steel Cut Oats)
    2 tablespoons flaxseed powder

1. Bring water and salt to a boil. Then add steel-cut oats.

2. Reduce heat to a simmer. Cover and cook 10 to 20 minutes (depending on what consistency you like your oatmeal to be). Stir occasionally.

3. Remove from heat and let stand covered for a couple of minutes.

4. Mix in flaxseed powder.

Quick and Easy Salads

Koko's Kale
Serves 2

I love this hearty salad with a classic balsamic vinaigrette.

1 grilled or roasted chicken breast

1 large bunch kale (about 10 ounces)

1 cup chopped cherry tomatoes

2–3 ounces goat cheese

½ avocado, pitted and sliced

⅓ cup dry-roasted almonds

BALSAMIC VINAIGRETTE

3 tablespoons balsamic vinegar

½ cup olive oil

1 garlic clove, minced

Pinch sea salt

Freshly ground black pepper

1 tablespoon Dijon mustard (optional)

1. Finely chop or shred the chicken.

2. In a large bowl, combine the chicken, kale, tomatoes, goat cheese, avocado, and almonds.

3. In a small bowl, combine all dressing ingredients and whisk thoroughly.

4. Toss the dressing with the salad or serve the dressing on the side.

Kucumber Krazed
Serves 2

This delicious and refreshing salad is my summer go-to meal. The lemon vinaigrette gives it a tangy zing!

- 1 grilled or roasted chicken breast
- 2 cucumbers, sliced
- 1 cup chopped tomatoes
- ½ cup crumbled feta
- ¼ sliced red onion
- ⅓ cup pitted and chopped black olives

LEMON VINAIGRETTE

- ½ teaspoon finely grated lemon zest
- 2 tablespoons freshly squeezed lemon juice
- ½ teaspoon Dijon mustard
- 3–4 tablespoons olive oil
- 1 small garlic clove, minced
- Pinch sea salt
- Freshly ground black pepper

1. Finely chop or shred the chicken.

2. In a large bowl, combine the chicken with the other salad ingredients.

3. In a small bowl, combine all dressing ingredients and whisk thoroughly.

4. Toss the salad with the lemon vinaigrette and salt and pepper to taste. The dressing may also be served on the side.

Chinese Chicken Salad
Serves 2

The light sesame ginger dressing goes perfectly with this Asian-inspired salad.

2 cups shredded romaine lettuce

1 cup shredded cabbage

2 scallions, finely chopped

1 large carrot, shredded or finely chopped

1 handful cilantro, chopped

½ avocado, pitted and chopped

2 cups shredded chicken

¼ cup peanuts, roughly chopped, for serving

LIGHT SESAME GINGER DRESSING

3 tablespoons sesame oil

1 teaspoon soy sauce

3 tablespoons rice vinegar

1 tablespoon honey

1 tablespoon toasted sesame seeds

1½-inch piece fresh ginger, peeled and minced

1. In a large bowl, combine all the salad ingredients.

2. In a small bowl, combine all dressing ingredients and whisk thoroughly.

3. Toss the salad with the dressing or leave the dressing on the side.

4. Sprinkle with peanuts.

Fruit Fanatic
Serves 2

One of the amazing things about California is that you can get great strawberries during much of the year. The combination of the strawberries and the light tang of the glaze in this simple recipe is awesome. If you want, you can add grilled chicken to this salad, too.

10 ounces baby spinach, rinsed and roughly chopped
1 quart fresh strawberries, cleaned, hulled, and sliced
2 ounces Gorgonzola crumbles
¼ cup candied walnuts
½ cup sliced red grapes

BALSAMIC GLAZE

1½ cups balsamic vinegar
1 tablespoon brown sugar or honey

1. In a large bowl, combine the salad ingredients.

2. To make the glaze, mix the balsamic vinegar with the brown sugar in a nonreactive saucepan over medium heat. Stir until the sugar has dissolved.

3. Bring to a boil, then reduce the heat to low and simmer until the glaze is reduced by half. It will take about 10 to 15 minutes to thicken and reduce, but be careful not to burn it near the end!

3. Pour the glaze into a jar and let it cool.

4. Drizzle the balsamic glaze over the fruit. Remember, a little goes a long way!

I had the pleasure of shooting the photos for this book at One Gun Ranch, the gorgeous home of Alice Bamford and Ann Eysenring, the authors of *The Malibu Biodynamic Diet*.

Grilled Goddess
Serves 2

To change things up, substitute grilled shrimp for the chicken.

1 zucchini, cut crosswise into ¼-inch thick slices

5 asparagus spears

1 bell pepper, cut into strips

1 red onion, cut into ¼-inch thick rings

½ eggplant, thinly sliced into rounds

Sea salt

Freshly ground black pepper

2 cups baby greens

1 grilled chicken breast, sliced

Olive oil

Juice of 1 lemon

1. Lightly grease the grill with some oil and heat to medium-high.

2. Place the zucchini, bell pepper, red onion, and eggplant on the grill and sprinkle on some salt and pepper.

3. Turn the vegetables once. Grill until they are slightly charred and cooked through, about 20 minutes.

4. Combine the grilled vegetables with the baby greens and chicken.

5. Toss with a dash of olive oil, a squeeze of lemon, and salt and pepper to taste

Mixed Greens with Roasted Brussels Sprouts and Lemon Dijon Vinaigrette
Serves 3–4

You can add sliced grilled chicken, salmon, or hard-boiled egg to this salad for an extra protein punch.

4 cups mixed greens

2–3 cups Brussels sprouts, sliced

Extra-virgin olive oil

Sea salt

Freshly ground black pepper

¼–⅓ cup pine nuts

1 red bell pepper

1 avocado, pitted and peeled

¼ cup chopped green onions

DRESSING

¼ cup white wine vinegar

⅛ cup balsamic vinegar

¼ cup extra-virgin olive oil

½ tablespoon Dijon mustard

Juice of ½ lemon

Sea salt

Freshly ground black pepper

1. Preheat the oven to 400°F.

2. Rinse the mixed greens and set aside in a large bowl.

3. Cut Brussels sprouts into quarters. Place in a bowl and add ⅛ cup extra-virgin olive oil. Add salt and pepper to taste. Mix and coat the Brussels sprouts thoroughly. Place on a cookie tray or baking dish and spread them out evenly. Roast in the oven for 20 to 25 minutes. If you'd like them well done, leave them in for an extra 10 to 15 minutes. When roasted to desired taste, remove and set aside.

4. On a separate cookie sheet or baking dish, evenly spread out the pine nuts. Toast in the oven for 5 to 10 minutes, depending on your oven. (If your oven is large enough, you can toast the nuts at the same time as you roast the Brussels sprouts.) Keep an eye on the nuts, as they tend to burn quickly. When toasted to desired taste, remove and set aside.

5. Seed and chop the red pepper and slice the avocado to desired size.

6. Add the Brussels sprouts, pine nuts, bell pepper, avocado, and green onions to the mixed greens.

7. In a small bowl, combine all the dressing ingredients and whisk thoroughly. Toss the salad with the dressing or leave the dressing on the side.

Mixed Greens with Goat Cheese and Dried Cranberries with Garlic Vinaigrette
Serves 3–4

Sliced grilled chicken, salmon, or cooked ground turkey can be added for a protein punch.

- ¼–⅓ cup pine nuts
- ½ cup cherry tomatoes
- ⅓ cup Kalamata olives
- 1 red bell pepper
- 1 cucumber
- ¼ cup goat cheese (optional; may also substitute vegan cheese)
- ¼ cup unsweetened dried cranberries
- ¼–⅓ cup pine nuts
- 4 cups mixed greens

GARLIC VINAIGRETTE DRESSING

- ⅛ cup red wine vinegar
- ⅛ cup balsamic vinegar
- ¼ cup extra-virgin olive oil
- ½ teaspoon fresh crushed garlic
- ½ teaspoon sugar or agave nectar (optional)

1. Preheat oven to 400°F. On a cookie sheet or baking dish, evenly spread pine nuts. Toast in the oven for 5 to 10 minutes, or until nuts reach desired brownness. Keep an eye on them, as they tend to burn quickly. Remove and set aside.

2. Slice cherry tomatoes, olives, red pepper, and cucumber to desired size.

3. In large bowl, combine the tomatoes, olives, red pepper, cucumber, goat cheese (if desired), cranberries, and toasted pine nuts with the mixed greens.

4. In a small bowl, combine all dressing ingredients and whisk thoroughly. You may add a little sugar or agave to cut the dressing if preferred. Toss the salad with the dressing or leave the dressing on the side.

Lentil Salad
Serves 2

This delicious salad is best served chilled.

2 Persian cucumbers

1 Granny Smith apple

¼ cup fresh cilantro

½–1 jalapeño (optional)

2 cups cooked lentils

¼ cup extra-virgin olive oil

Sea salt

Freshly ground black pepper

1. Slice cucumbers and cut each slice into quarters. Core and dice apple. Finely chop cilantro. If you'd like a little extra heat, finely chop jalapeño.

2. In a large bowl, combine the lentils with the cucumbers, apple, cilantro, and jalapeño.

3. Add olive oil to salad, salt and pepper to taste, and toss.

Steamed Veggies and Fish
Serves 1

1 head broccoli or cauliflower, cut into florets

1 zucchini, cut into ½-inch rounds

Sea salt

Freshly ground black pepper

1 lemon, halved

1 8-ounce skinless whitefish fillet (about 1 inch thick)

2 teaspoons extra-virgin olive oil

2 tablespoons finely chopped fresh herbs (I like basil and parsley)

1. Place a steamer basket in a large saucepan. Add enough water to reach just below the bottom of the steamer. Bring water to a boil.

2. Add the vegetables and steam, covered, until soft, about 7 minutes.

3. Add a pinch of salt, pepper, and a squeeze of lemon to the fish.

4. Place fish on the steamer, cover, and cook until it flakes easily and is the same color throughout, about 7 minutes.

5. Drizzle the fish and vegetables with the oil. Sprinkle with the herbs and serve with a squeeze of lemon.

Who says healthy food can't be fun? These recipes taste better than the real thing!

Fake It Till You Bake It
Serves 4–6

Enjoy French fries with a fraction of the fat and carbs!

3 whole jicamas or turnips

Coconut oil (to spray)

Olive oil

Spices of your choice (salt, pepper, garlic powder, onion powder . . . or get crazy with a dash of paprika!)

1. Preheat the oven to 425°F.

2. Line a baking sheet with aluminum foil and spray with coconut oil.

3. Peel and cut jicama or turnip into fry-like sticks.

4. Place in a large bowl and toss with olive oil to coat. Spice it up!

5. Spread the "fries" on the prepared baking sheet and bake until crispy (about 20 minutes); flip over halfway through.

Magic Mash-Up
Serves 3–4

Better than mashed potatoes!

  1 large head cauliflower
  1 tablespoon olive oil
  Sea salt
  Freshly ground black pepper
  1 garlic clove, chopped
  Chopped chives

1. Separate the cauliflower into florets.

2. Bring 1 cup of water to simmer in a pot and add the cauliflower. Cover and turn the heat to medium. Cook the cauliflower until very tender, about 12 to 15 minutes.

3. Drain well, reserving ¼ cup of the cooking water.

4. Add olive oil, a pinch of salt and pepper, garlic, and chives to taste. Mash the cauliflower with a potato masher until it resembles mashed potatoes, adding 1 tablespoon of water at a time if necessary for consistency.

Homemade Hummus

Add some pita chips, and you've got my favorite snack.

   2 cups canned garbanzo beans, drained

   ⅓ cup tahini

   3 tablespoons lemon juice

   2 garlic cloves

   1 teaspoon salt

   3 teaspoons olive oil

   Pinch of cumin

1. Place all ingredients into the bowl of a food processor or a blender.

2. Puree until smooth.

3. Enjoy!

I Dream of Ice Cream
Serves 2

2 ripe bananas, peeled, chopped, and frozen

Handful of blackberries

Dash of almond milk

1 tablespoon walnuts or almonds.

Dash stevia

1. Place ripe bananas, almond milk, nuts, and stevia in the bowl of a food processor and process until smooth.

2. Top your "ice cream" with extra walnuts or almonds.

3. Voilà!

Finally, I'd like to end this section by urging you to cut loose and celebrate once in a while. You deserve it after all those sweaty work-outs. It's not *always* about health. Sometimes you want something because you love it, like my breaded chicken. It's a very simple recipe and quick to prepare. The chicken is really good, and it won't last. Whenever I have company, people request my breaded chicken. I always make twice as much as I think I'm going to need, and my guests gobble up all I've made and want more. I've never once had leftover chicken. Fix some yourself. You'll see.

Khloé's Famous Breaded Chicken
Serves 4

4 boneless, skinless chicken breasts

2 eggs

1 cup flour

½ cup bread crumbs

½ cup crushed Ritz crackers

Lawry's seasoned salt

Lawry's garlic salt

Black pepper

4 tablespoons unsalted butter

1. Preheat the oven to 350°F.

2. Wash the chicken breasts well and pat them dry with paper towels.

3 In a small bowl, beat the eggs.

4. In another small bowl, mix the flour, bread crumbs, crushed Ritz crackers, salts, and black pepper together.

5. Dip the chicken breasts one at a time first in the beaten eggs and then in the flour mixture.

6. Place the chicken breasts in a Pyrex dish and add lots of chunks of butter. Bake, uncovered, in the oven for about 50 minutes, or until juices run clear when pierced with a fork.

In the spirit of occasionally indulging and in honor of my new TV show, I present this next section on Kocktails with Khloé.

Kocktails with Khloé

The Kris Jenner
Serves 1

This famous Kris Jenner is a straight shooter. It is her go-to that always does the trick. We call this Mom's Personality Juice.

Belvedere Vodka
Diet tonic or soda water
Limes

1. Fill a Baccarat highball glass with ice to the very top.

2. Fill the glass halfway with Mom's beloved Belvedere Vodka.

3. Top the glass with diet tonic or soda water (depending on Mom's mood).

4. Squeeze two wedges of lime into the beverage and throw them in there for extra oomph.

5. Strain the mix into a glass with ice.

6. Garnish the drink with a mint sprig and a watermelon wedge.

Elderflower Champagne Pitcher
Serves 8

1 cup fresh strawberries

1 bottle Champagne

1 cup elderflower liqueur

12 ounces club soda

1. Wash and stem the fresh strawberries.

2. Add the Champagne, elderflower liqueur, and club soda to a large pitcher. Stir well.

3. Add strawberries.

4. Serve and enjoy!

Water-Minty-Melon
Serves 1

2 fresh mint leaves

1½ ounces premium vodka

1½ ounces fresh watermelon juice

¼ teaspoon agave syrup

Sprig mint (for garnish)

Small wedge watermelon (for garnish)

1. Rip the mint in half to release its flavor and throw into a shaker.

2. Add vodka, juice, and agave syrup.

3. Shake with ice.

I also love this one without the vodka. You can just serve the delicious watermelon juice with mint and a splash of club soda for the fizz.

Part 2

MIND

Chapter 3
Get Your Head on Straight

Strengthening my body strengthened my mind, but it is also true that you need a strong mind to get a strong body. The thing about making changes in your body is that you can't do it without getting lots of help from your mind. You need discipline and awareness and dedication. From time to time, your mind is going to refuse to help you, and you'll stumble, maybe even fall, but there's always tomorrow. Not making it to the gym for two or three days in a row is not fatal, but it's a mistake, and you need to get your mind right. There's a great quote about this: *The first time is a mistake. The second time is a choice.*

Let me give you an example of one of my bigger mistakes.

My father, Robert Kardashian, passed away on September 30, 2003. I was nineteen at the time, and to say I didn't handle his death well is an understatement. I didn't turn to drugs, but I certainly drowned my sorrows in drink, and the partying soon got out of hand. I was underage and behaving recklessly in clubs and at private parties, and I found myself surrounded by people who didn't have my best interests at heart. It was pretty much "Don't worry. We can get you into this club." Or "Here, have one more drink for the road." Or "It's too early to go home. Let's hit so-and-so's house. He really knows how to throw a party."

Looking back on this period these many years later, I realize that I was doing what most of us do: trying to avoid my pain by numbing it. (In my opinion, this is the source of almost all addictions.) And in fact during this period I became aware of how easy it is to become a binge drinker and a binge eater. I see pictures of myself at the time and I was so bloated that I look like I'm forty-five years old!

I also pulled away from the people who were closest to me, distancing myself from my family. It was the first time in my life I had ever done anything like that, and they were very concerned, but being around them served only to remind me of my father, and I found that too painful.

I wasn't strong enough to handle the pain or to get help—from my family, friends, or even myself.

The Queen of Denial

I still remember the day Kourtney called to break the news about his death. We'd all been expecting it, of course, but it was still a shock. She reached me at my apartment and said, "Dad passed away." And I was hysterical for about two or three minutes. Then I stopped screaming and went into the bathroom and started doing my makeup.

My best friend, Malika, was there, with her twin sister, and both of them were really concerned. They didn't understand why I was so calm. Easy: I had gone into total denial. I was thinking, "My dad didn't really die." I asked them to invite some friends over, and they weren't sure it was a good idea. "Is that what you really want?" Malika asked. "Yes," I said. "*Yes.*" And that's how I got through the first night. By having friends over and drinking and snacking and acting as if Kourtney had never called. I didn't even cry.

At the funeral, though, when I saw my father in his casket, I completely fell apart. I don't remember the details, but apparently I was an emotional wreck, and I'm told that I was so distraught I actually passed out. At one point I fell to the floor kicking and screaming, and I had to be sedated. It was really intense. I refused to believe my father was gone. I wanted to believe it was all just a bad dream.

That's when the partying started. Again, my refusal to accept my father's death turned me into the *definition* of denial.

People would approach to express their condolences, and I would brush them off. "What are you talking about? I'm fine. Everything's great!" I was so fragile that I was scared to even acknowledge what had really happened, because to acknowledge the truth was to feel unbearable pain.

Just as my life was beginning to spiral completely out of control, my family came to the rescue. My mom and Kourtney had a store called Smooch, and the space next door had just been vacated, so she took over the lease and decided we were going to open a woman's boutique and call it DASH. She came to me and said, "Khloé, you're going to be running this store. Don't worry. We're going to figure things out." Actually, to be honest, she was a bit more blunt. It seemed harsh at the time, sure, but it was exactly what I needed. She is the oldest of my sisters and the most level-headed, and she took it upon herself to turn me around.

The only previous retail experience I'd had was when I was

sixteen and had worked in a clothing store, so clearly I had a lot to learn. But as soon as I started, I loved it! It was such a healthy way to deal with my sorrow. Just getting up, going to work, and being productive changed my entire outlook on life. I still missed my father, of course, and there were times when I cried myself to sleep at night, but I knew I would survive.

At the time, Kourtney was living in a townhouse in Calabasas, and she asked me to move in with her. She sort of conned me a little. "You'll save on rent. It's close to the store. And it'll be fun to live together." Because I was still a teenager, I was a little rebellious and wanted my independence, but the truth is, it was nice to be taken under my sister's wing, to be pulled back into the family again. I missed that connection, so I'm grateful that Kourtney took me by the hand and led me back to the fold.

You Need a Reason to Get Out of Bed

The fact that I had to go to work every day made a huge difference. I learned the importance of *purpose* and *structure*. I had responsibilities at the store, and that made me feel good. And I was so busy I didn't even have time to think, which isn't a bad thing. It's a form of escape, sure, but it's a *productive* escape. There were days when we hardly had time for lunch. One of us would grab takeout and we'd eat while we talked about our day: how sales were going, which items seemed to sell best, whether we should change the window display—stuff like that. It was an exciting time. We had started the business together, and it was already beginning to take off. Plus every morning when I opened my eyes I had a reason to get out of bed. People lose sight of that. *You need a reason to get out of bed*, whether you're going to a job or the gym or taking care of your kids. A life without structure is too risky. A life without structure is the road to collapse. When I look at my friends who live without structure, and at that own chaotic period in my life, I understand how easy it is to lose control of your life. You've got to hold on tight to those reins. You have to be in control. You are responsible for your own happiness.

When I look back on those booze-fueled nights that preceded the turnaround, I'm almost embarrassed. The whole experience was so *sloppy*. I'd stumble into bed and wake up in a fog that lasted well into the next day, and in the evening I'd start all over again. It defied comprehension. I remember thinking, "This is no fun. Why am I doing this to myself? I feel like shit." But I couldn't find the strength to stop.

I didn't end up in rehab or anything, because Kourtney put her foot down and forced me to take control of my life, but I probably came close. And I am still mystified by the appeal of alcohol: It didn't make me feel any better, it didn't fix anything, but I kept going back for more. Crazy, huh? It's like that definition of madness: *You keep doing the exact same thing over and over again, expecting a different result.* That was definitely me.

On the other hand, just to clarify, I am not anti-drinking. I think drinking *in moderation* is fine, and—if you believe the science—might even have some health benefits. But drinking to deal with your problems is not the way to go. And anyone who drinks and loses control— well, I know from personal experience that this is not a pretty sight.

Still, for me, this period was very scary, and now I'm all about staying in control. Then again, I've also come to terms with the fact that life is unpredictable. You're pretty sure you know what's coming five minutes from now and what's going to happen tomorrow, but sometimes you're just plain wrong. Is it scary? Sure, sometimes. Is it unpleasant? On occasion, absolutely. But that unpredictable quality also makes life interesting and exciting, and I've learned to embrace the unexpected. Nowadays I tell myself, "Whatever happens, I'll deal with it." And I do. Partly because I have a good mind-set, and partly because there is no other choice. This is life. Shit happens. You could put on a crash helmet and lock yourself in a padded room and maybe you'd be a little *safer*, if that's what you want to call it, but who wants such a boring, lonely life? Not me. One of the reasons life is exciting is because it throws lots of shit at you, and whether your experiences are good or bad is ultimately determined by the way you deal with those surprises, unpleasant and otherwise.

Now, to be completely honest, I wouldn't have said the same

thing years ago. Three years ago, I was looking for stability and pre-dictability. I was worried about my so-called five-year plan, because I didn't have one. But now I realize that I actually thrive on chaos. I think all of the Kardashians do. We like drama because it's like a shot of adrenaline. We like problems because suddenly we have another opportunity to find a smart solution. I think this is a much healthier way to approach daily life. You can and should try to impose order on your life—get a job, pay those bills, etc.—but you shouldn't freak out when the unexpected happens. People who are obsessed with control are the first ones to lose control when something doesn't go their way.

Certainly you are the captain of your own ship. And you have to steer it. But things are never going to come together exactly as you imagined. Take a look at your goals. Open your eyes to other op-portunities. Get involved with your community and with the world around you. If you're not excited about your life, it's up to you to make your life exciting. It's one thing to be laid back and another thing entirely to push yourself, and I belong to the latter category. I believe you have to be your own engine, find your own purpose, but I started figuring that out only when I began working at DASH. The job gave me purpose and direction. *Work changed my life.*

I remember talking to a friend about this and he told me that life was a lot like being on a bike; if you're standing still, it's really hard to maintain your balance. But if you're moving forward, you don't even have to think about it. The bike pretty much balances itself. And that is absolutely true.

Plus I found that people are more attracted to you when you're healthy and productive. Everyone wants to get on the train when it's moving, but no one is interested when it's stopped. I had gone from an inactive, purposeless life to one that was productive and exciting and full of promise. All because I was working.

Well, maybe not *all*. The other important thing I learned from the experience was that I'd made the mistake of trying to outrun my pain, when what I really needed to do was face it. If you don't face your pain, it will have a terrible hold over you. But once you acknowledge it, you come to understand that it is neither as powerful nor as terrifying as you imagined.

That was over a decade ago, and a great deal has changed since, but I know one thing for certain: I am never going to make that same mistake again. Alcohol and drugs don't hold any appeal for me. Life is about choice, and the right choice tends to be the harder choice, but it's worth it.

Somebody once said, "Suffering is not caused by pain, but by *resisting* pain." I couldn't agree more.

Now I know what you're thinking. *Sometimes we're in a place in life where it's really hard to get motivated. And we might not be lucky enough to have a sister come to our rescue. Plus many of us don't have jobs that excite us.* And you know what? All of that is valid, but it doesn't change reality: Each of us is the architect of our own future. Each of us is responsible for finding our own way.

And sure, motivation can be a real bitch, but you won't get strong without it. In my own life, two elements that are really critical are *structure* and *routine*, and knowing that keeps me motivated. I start my day with my workout because that lays the foundation for everything that follows. I get my heart pumping. I sweat. I feel good. And I use all of that good energy to put a positive spin on my entire day.

If I miss my morning workout, it doesn't exactly ruin my day, but somehow I don't feel complete. I like to start the day strong, and sometimes I end it strong, too—by running over to Equinox in the early evening for thirty minutes on the treadmill. Not a bad

The most effective way to do it, is to do it.

—Amelia Earhart

way to end the day! A little alone time, half an hour of exercise, and reflection.

Of course, like everyone else, I have mornings when I feel completely blah and don't even want to get out of bed. I force myself to get up, drink my big glass of water, have my coffee, and start moving. And while the schedule isn't the issue—some people are happier going for a run at the end of the day, when they get home from work—I do think structure and consistency are critically important. That way you know what's expected of you, or more specifically, what you're expecting of yourself, and you're more likely to follow through.

So for me it's all about the morning, waking up motivated. I'm going to Gunnar's. I'm going to sweat. Then I'm going to go home and shower and get ready for work. And that motivation carries over. I approach work with the same energy that I approach the gym, feeling *fueled* by my time at the gym, and that's no accident—it's learned behavior.

And here's the thing: I love work. When I was drinking, doing nothing, I felt like an unproductive nobody. But when I work, I feel energized and alive.

Work: The Great Escape

Work has plenty of other benefits, too. When you're busy, your problems tend to fade into the background. I had things to do. I was busy. I was focused. I knew I still had problems, of course, and that they were waiting for me at home, but work took me away from them for a period of time, and I was grateful for that. I discovered that the best therapy is to be busy and productive. It seems to rewire your brain. It's as if the lights go back on.

A day
of worry
is more
exhausting
than a week
of work.

—John Lubbock

That's why I'm very goal-oriented. I think it's important to look for purpose every day, whether that's at an office or at home. I'm especially in awe of stay-at-home moms. A stay-at-home mom has to keep a lot of balls in the air and rarely gets a moment for herself—she's getting everyone up and ready, clothed and fed, she's making sure the house runs smoothly. That gives her purpose. She's busy. And while some women might not find those domestic responsibilities all that exciting, I bet they still realize how necessary their work is, and I have a feeling that this is a reward in and of itself. (I know it was for me, back when I was a stepmom.) The point is, you have to find something for *you*, something that excites *you*. And it could be as simple as—and admittedly I'm biased here—a membership at your local gym.

If you put out positive energy, if you're moving and grooving, the wheels on that bike are going to take you in all sorts of new and exciting directions. And even when I experience low-energy days (because I have those, too), I look for a way to make my life exciting. *How can I challenge myself today? What do I need to do here to switch gears?*

All it takes is a little willpower. Like with my sister Kourtney, who works really hard to take care of her family but no matter what is going on makes sure that she gets out of bed and goes to see her trainer. Her trainer is impressed by her dedication. "It's good you showed up," he tells her. "Most people would have used this as an excuse not to exercise, when this is in fact the time in your life that you need it most." I couldn't agree more. That's part of the formula for success. When things get tough, you get tougher. As I told Kourtney, "Exercise saved me."

We're all allowed to have a bad day from time to time, but

there's a limit. Inactivity and depression feed on themselves. The more you wallow, the worse it gets. But energy is the opposite of depression. It's like a powerful motor that's going to move you exactly where you need to be.

People get into ruts for lots of reasons. A lot of women, for example, get into a really bad place right after they have babies. They're exhausted, the constant breastfeeding really takes it out of them, and their bodies are changing radically. They find it almost impossible to look and feel great. It's hard even to keep their clothes presentable; everything they wear ends up dirty—spit up, diaper explosions, leaking milk. After your baby is born, your body is recovering from trauma, you are exhausted, and your life is constrained by the baby's needs. Your shoulders, back, and neck ache. It's hard to give yourself the chance to feel good, even for a few minutes. But even a tiny effort can change that. You get up, you shower, and you wash your hair. The transformation is instant. Or when your baby is doing tummy time, you can get down on the floor and stretch or do a few simple exercises—taking the time to tend to the muscles that ache. Or you bundle your baby up and go for a short walk. You look better and you *feel* better.

Of course, all the sacrifices you make as a parent are *beyond* worth it. You are shaping the life of a little human being! I haven't had that experience *yet*, but I am looking forward to it because I can't imagine *anything* in life compares to the miracle of motherhood.

And I have my own bad days (not yet related to the demands of motherhood, of course). For example, when I'm sick, I have a hard time getting motivated. I mean, if I'm truly sick, I'm probably not going to hit the gym, but if I'm just a *little* sick, I might go for a brisk walk. I want to get that blood pumping, one way or another. I like to feel that sweat oozing out of my pores. And no matter how sick

I am, I always, always, always take a shower. Just being clean makes me feel better. People who focus on being sick make themselves sicker. If your body tells you not to get out of bed, listen to it. But you also need to listen when it's telling you to get your ass in gear.

I'm lucky in that I have such a large, loving family. And while I tend to be more introverted than the others, less inclined to share, I also know that they are always there for me. In my family we have a saying: *Two heads are better than one, and three heads are better than two.* We're not just looking out for ourselves; we're a team, watching out for one another. We challenge one another and it keeps us fresh and alert. And we feel secure with one another, which helps us make better, bolder decisions.

Also, I've learned from my mom that you have to fight for the things you believe in. For example, she met Bruce before her divorce was final, and they were crazy about each other, so Bruce went to see my father to ask him to please hurry things along so he and my mother could get married. Bruce also told him that they weren't interested in his money.

As soon as the papers were signed, Bruce and my mother got married, and not long afterward, they realized they were broke. Bruce was a motivational speaker at the time, but the business was basically treading water, and my mom decided she was going to change that. She got on the phone and began booking Bruce into any venue that would take him, no matter how small or how low the pay, and she simultaneously helped him create a series of workout videos (in which she costarred, naturally). She pushed and pushed until at long last Coca-Cola and Visa came calling. And that, as they say, changed everything.

And this was back in the days before the Internet! Zero social media! My mother did everything on the phone or via snail mail. She had a Rolodex! (And if you don't know what that is, check it out on the Web. You won't believe how our parents used to live, LOL. It's a miracle they survived!)

Now, many years later, my mother likes to joke that Bruce was her first major project, and that we children came next. But the point is, she didn't curl up in a fetal position and give up, even when things were at their lowest point. She fought like hell. Actions speak louder than words. I have learned so much about strength from my mother. Even during the toughest times in her life, she carried herself with dignity and strength, and she knew that the only person who could save her life was herself.

I was only six years old when she and Bruce got married, so of course I don't remember the details, but years later, when I heard the story—and I've heard it many times—it was a great source of inspiration. Knowing that story, and being a product of the result, I don't need anyone to tell me how important it is to get motivated. On the contrary, I learned early that without motivation you are lost. And how do you get motivated? Well, it's actually pretty simple and boils down to two choices. One, you can sit here in the dark, crying. Or two, you can come to grips with the fact that nobody is going to do it for you and make a commitment to change.

Bruce is the first one to tell you that my mother turned his life around. When she met him, his Olympic gold medal was sitting at the bottom of his underwear drawer, and he was struggling to motivate *himself*, let alone others. This is a problem for anyone, and a huge problem for a motivational speaker. But Mom came along and built a fire under his ass, and the rest is history.

People look at our extended clan, the Jenner Kardashians, and they see an empire. And while it's true that we've had more opportunities than most people, we've had to fight hard, too. People love to discredit the hard work we have put into succeeding and keeping all of our trains moving steadily. And even when you get to a good place, which is an achievement in and of itself, it's challenging to maintain the success.

Khlo-$ ("Khlo Money")

As long as we're on the subject, I'll say this about money: It's great, but it's not the answer. I know people who have more money than they could possibly spend in a lifetime, and they're not happy. And I know that a good part of the reason is that they've lost their motivation. They made it. They've got the big house and the fancy cars

and even the private plane. There's nothing left to work for, and they find that doing nothing leaves them empty.

We are propelled through life by our hopes and dreams, but we also have to deal with reality. The trick is not to let reality get in the way. There will be setbacks, disappointment, and heartbreak, but the dream will keep you going. Believe in yourself and the dreams will come true.

I love what Jim Carrey said: "I think everybody should get rich and famous and do everything they have ever dreamed of so they can see that it's not the answer."

Life is about forward motion. You have to keep moving. It's up to each of us to move in the right direction. No excuses. Stop wasting your time and energy by discrediting the hard work and dedication of other people. So what if they had more opportunities than you? If they had *fewer* opportunities, how would that change *your* situation? Focus your passion and energy on your own goals.

I have a lot of friends who talk a good game. They're, like, "Oh, I want a great job," or "I'm so tired of this lifestyle." Or they get a little jealous when they see my new car. But the thing is, they're not doing anything to get that job or that lifestyle or that car. There is no action there. Some of them are my age and older and they still act like high school kids. I remember when I was in high school, I actually got a credit card from Victoria's Secret, with a $500 limit, and I immediately went out and spent the entire limit. By the end of the month, I was being asked to pay it back, and I didn't have the money to pay it back—I was a kid!—and was also too embarrassed to ask my parents, so that unpaid bill haunted me for the next three years (and to this day has affected my credit score). I was seventeen at the time, and I dealt with the situation with all the maturity of a seventeen-year-old, but I know too many thirty-year-olds who still behave like confused teens. What is that about? At some point you have to deal with adult-hood and everything it entails. You have to pay your bills. You have to get health insurance, even if it feels like a monumental waste of money. And yes, you have to file a tax return every year. But I have friends who come crying to me because they're in debt or have no health insurance or are in trouble with the Internal Revenue Service because they *have never filed a tax return.*

As you mature, you have to take on greater responsibilities. It's your life, and no one can live it for you. No one can organize it for you, either. Take care of the little things before the little things take over your life.

People ask me all the time, "Why do you guys work so much? You could retire." And in fact I got that a lot after Lamar and I were married; he was making a lot of money and people couldn't un-derstand why I remained so driven. I remember one of my friends saying, "Why don't you just become a housewife?"

And I told her: "I *am* a housewife. And I think I'm a pretty good one. But I want my own identity. I want to make my own way and my own money. And I want a good reason to get out of bed in the morning."

Beyond that, though, and even more important, I want to be productive. I know many housewives, mothers, and homemakers who are completely fulfilled in their lives, and I salute them, but I'm wired a little differently; I'm one of those women who wants it all, absolutely, but I want it *in balance.* I'll take everything life has to offer, and then some. I like to drop into bed at the end of the day with a happy sigh, thinking, "What a great day. I accomplished so much."

Now, I'm the first to admit that I didn't do it alone. I have a tremendously loyal family. They are there for me every day, and they were there to lend a helping hand when I was in a deep, dark place.

think about what you have

I'm super grateful because they have always believed in me, even in my darkest hours. But nothing good would have come of their efforts if I hadn't believed in myself, and at the end of the day, that's what it boils down to for us all. Success is about doing the work even when you don't feel like it, and often *especially* when you don't feel like it.

To me, working is not that different from working out. When you work out, your body changes, and you feel good about those changes. When you work, you feel a sense of accomplishment, especially if you're lucky enough to be doing meaningful work. If not, at least your bank balance changes, and you feel good about *that*. After all, when you have money in the bank, you don't have to worry about *not* having money in the bank! And that makes everything worthwhile, right?

Wired to Be Good

If you don't have a supportive family or a network of good friends, things will of course be a little more challenging, but you can be proactive and change that. You can get involved in the community, take classes, do volunteer work. I know people who spend their days trying to figure out how to help others, and it makes you wonder whether some people are just wired to be good. But one of my friends explained it to me. "When I volunteer, I feel really good about myself," she said. "So in a strange way, it's a selfish act. The more I do for others, the better I feel about my own life."

I thought that was amazing. She herself is enriched by her generosity. If she is being "selfish," she has found the perfect way to do it. That story reminded me of my father, who was a self-made millionaire at twenty-one, but who still made us help out at soup kitchens when we were young. He used to say, "We are very lucky. You should never forget that. As you go through life, you should always look for opportunities to help people who aren't as lucky as you."

From my father, I learned that there are basically three ways to be charitable. One is to donate your time, as we did when we were young. Another is to write a check to a deserving organization, which I still do, but privately. And the third is to help the people around you, people who will genuinely benefit from your generosity. This last method is my favorite. When dealing with charitable organizations, I worry about where my contribution is going. You hear terrible stories about organizations that use ninety cents out of every dollar to cover salaries for the executives, and that only ten cents—if that—actually gets to the people who need the money. But if a friend needs a loan to go to college, or has to get her car fixed in order to get to work, or has a health problem, and I can help

Do right. Do your best. Treat others as you want to be treated.

—Lou Holtz

that person. I do what I can, within reason, and I feel good both for my friend and for myself.

As far as donating my time, however, that's no longer in the cards. Can you imagine what would happen if the Kardashians showed up at a soup kitchen, ready to serve? It would be bedlam, with paparazzi and news crews jostling for the best shots.

But really, to give is to receive, no matter how you do it. That's something to think about when you're feeling disconnected and alone.

Good Values and Good Habits Can Be Learned

For me, success in life really boils down to developing good habits. We talked about structure, about getting on that bike, about having purpose, but even the lesser habits add up to a healthy whole.

When I was around fourteen and on my summer break, my mother would come into my room every morning at seven and wake me up. I was, like, "Mom! Why do I have to get up this early?" And she would say, "You're not sleeping till noon. I don't care if it's summer. You need to get up every day and have *purpose*."

At the time I didn't understand this, and I found it immensely irritating. My friends stayed in bed till noon, and I was jealous. I would complain that I had nothing to do, and my mom would drag me along to wherever she was going. To a Tae Bo class. To the dry cleaner's. To Gunnar's gym. Grocery shopping. "You have to get out of the house," she would say. "You have to do something. Life is about being active, *alive*."

She did that with all of the kids except Kylie. Kylie was the youngest, and I guess she got a free pass because eventually parents get tired of pushing. Kylie often sleeps in, like a lot of teenagers, but it doesn't seem to have hurt her. And I think that's because she's

Things do
not happen.
Things are
made to
happen.

—John F. Kennedy

surrounded by a large and very hardworking family, so she gets the message every day.

I actually find myself unable to lounge in bed until all hours, thanks—or no thanks!—to my mom. I used to have a radio show and didn't get home till about 2:00 a.m., and that gave me a good excuse to sleep late, but even then I couldn't do it. I'd feel guilty. And if I had a houseguest, I'd feel both guilty and embarrassed. *That Khloé! My God. All she does is sleep!*

Those values—get up, seize the day—were ingrained at an early age, and I'm glad they were. But good values and good habits can be learned. Nobody taught me to go to the gym five days a week. I figured that out on my own. Try it. Set the alarm for 7:00 a.m. and you might be surprised by what you can accomplish in a single day.

Don't cheat yourself—treat yourself. When you don't take full advantage of your day, you are only shortchanging yourself. Think about it: Oprah has the exact same number of hours in her day as you do, and look at what she has done with them!

Getting your mind right has a lot of components, and most of them are about healthy habits. For example, I'm pretty obsessive about punctuality. I don't think there's any excuse for being late. I think it shows a flagrant disrespect for the other person's time.

Being late does not make you special or important, it makes you *unreliable*. Respect yourself enough to keep your word and your commitment to being prompt, whether in business or pleasure. If you agree on a time, stick to it.

This happens a lot when I meet friends for dinner. I ask them what time works, and they tell me, and we lock it in. And I'm always right on time—usually early, in fact—and they saunter in fifteen, twenty, even thirty minutes later. What is that about? Didn't we agree to meet at eight?

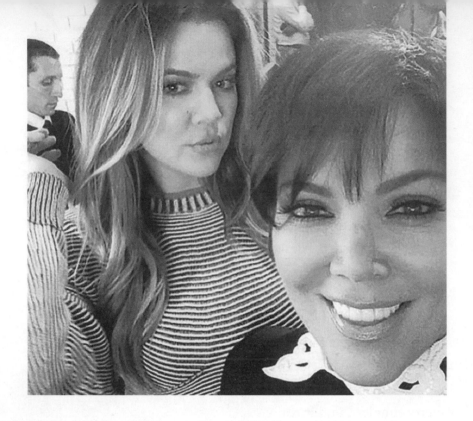

And it's interesting, because if it's about them—if, say, they're in therapy—they're always on time. How many people are late to their shrink? None. And you know why? Because they're going to talk about me, me, me, and they're going to make every minute count.

I respect other people's time and I think they should respect mine. This may seem like a small thing, but it's part of building a strong mind. It also speaks to *character* and *reputation*. Instead of becoming known as the late one, try to become the reliable one. Good habits are like exercise. The more you practice them, the stronger you get. And when people talk about me, I like to hear them talking about my strengths.

All of this basically boils down to respect. When you deal with others, be on time, follow through, keep your promises, and don't make excuses. Does it get any simpler than that?

Getting Organized

Another healthy habit relates to being organized. People are always complaining that they have too much to do and that there aren't enough hours in the day, but there are twenty-four hours in every day, for all of us, and it's really about making the most of them. (Do I need to bring up Oprah again?)

A great way to maximize your time is to make a to-do list. Early in my day, usually after my workout, I make a list of everything that needs to get done, and I get it done. For me, it's *visual*. When I see something written down, it's real. A solid list on paper is much more effective than a vague list in my head. I have a plan and I know exactly what I need to do to get through it.

And the main reason I'm motivated to complete my tasks is pretty simple: I find it really stressful when I *don't* complete them. Instead of worrying about everything I'm not getting done, I do it. It's really not that complicated. You do what you need to do when you need to do it, and then you move on to the next task.

Again, it's like working out. You do enough reps, you start getting strong. Before you know it, it's a habit, and you don't even have to think about it. You just focus and get it done.

If I make it sound easy, it's because it is. *Generally*. Because we all have days when we're not feeling it. But here's the thing: You can sit around and whine, or you can get on your bike and start pedaling. And make it a fun ride! If I have to clean out my garage, for example, I don't think, "I've wasted my entire Sunday!" Instead, I invite a few girlfriends over and lay out some healthy snacks (maybe a little wine, too) and we'll gossip our way through my chores. And if no one is available, there's always music. Haven't you ever cleaned house with Beyoncé or Michael Jackson blaring on the speakers?

Chapter 4
Make the Best of Everything

"No Whining" Zone

This brings me to the subject of whining, which I cannot tolerate. It's one thing to have a bad day, but chronic whining is toxic—for you and for everyone around you—so get it under control. Nobody likes to be around a Negative Nancy. It's contagious. If you're miserable, you don't have the right to impose your misery on the rest of the world.

We create the tone and circumstances of our lives by using the Law of Attraction. It is the principle by which all things manifest (or fail to manifest), and it affects every area of our lives. Negativity is seriously damaging. Now that you know that, doesn't it make sense to change the way you live?

I've often heard parents turn to their kids and say, "Stop whining!" Well, I wish we could do that with adults! Don't those whiners ever listen to themselves? It's like they are actually regressing—becoming little kids again—but they can't see it because they're as self-absorbed as children. (I hope you aren't one of those people, but if you are, change—quick!)

Not long ago I read an article about a group of people who signed up for an experiment: They wouldn't complain for an entire month. Researchers learned a lot from the study. When we complain, our brains release stress hormones that negatively impact our cognitive function. In other words, when you whine, your brain doesn't work as well. They also said that listening to someone moan and groan was as bad as secondhand smoke, which I found truly alarming. But here's what I learned from this study. First, avoid complainers. Second, turn your complaints into solutions. In other words, instead of sitting around obsessing about the problem, look for a way to change your situation.

I like to say, "You bring me problems, I'll give you solutions." I come from a place of yes, from a place of *We can do this, fix this, make it better*. Few things in life can't be fixed. And even if they can't be fixed, they can be made better.

Now please don't get me wrong. I like to think I'm a sympathetic, nurturing person, and my friends know they can rely on me when they hit a wall. We talk the situation through, look for a solution together, and move on. Nobody wants to be around a whiner. But whining is different from talking about a problem. Whining is unjustified self-pity. *I feel fat. I hate my hair. My boyfriend never brings me flowers.* Trust me, whining only makes things worse. Negativity begets negativity. How do you change it? By taking control. And you do that by taking one baby step at a time. It's sort of like doing reps, but in reverse. Today I'm going to make a concerted effort to whine less. Tomorrow I'll do even better. And within a week—miracle of miracles!—I hope not to be whining at all. See how it works? Not all that mysterious, is it?

One of my friends got married and moved away, and her life didn't turn out exactly like she'd hoped or expected. It happens. Her husband wasn't the man she thought he was, and she wasn't all that thrilled about being a wife and a homemaker, so it was unpleasant all around. When she first mentioned it to me, I suggested couples therapy, but she wasn't into that, and eventually I began to make other suggestions: Why don't you learn to cook? Why don't you take your husband on fun dates? Why don't you plan a romantic weekend getaway? But she did none of that; instead she kept whining until finally I got tired of it. "Look," I said, "every time you call me, all you do is complain, but I don't see you doing anything to make things better."

That didn't go over very well, so she began to unload on our other mutual friends, until they too got tired of her whining. And I'd like to tell you that this story has a happy ending, but it doesn't. She is still with her husband, and she is still miserable, and I imagine her husband is pretty miserable, too. But whose fault is that? Hers, of course. She hasn't been proactive. Everything we suggested fell on deaf ears. Instead of trying to change the situation, she blamed her husband and the town they had moved to and even the new people they met.

I don't mind trying to help my friends. On the contrary, it brings me joy. I also love the fact that they trust me enough to come to me with their problems. But I do mind people who look for help but won't try to help themselves.

Life is about moving forward. Blaming others and whining about your situation is about living in the past. Of course it doesn't work!

In our family, when something shitty happens, we are of course affected by it. But we deal with it and move on. It's water under the

bridge. And we even learn to laugh about it. If no one has been hurt, if there is no lasting damage, the best thing you can do is move on. And even if people are hurt, they can't be *unhurt*, so stop the woe-is-me crap and figure out how to deal with the situation.

Sometimes you have to laugh to keep from crying. And sometimes you have to learn to embrace even the bad things, because every experience shapes you, and some of the things you think of as bad may later turn out to be genuine blessings.

If you want to whine, here's my suggestion: Take out your journal and write down every little thing that comes into your head. Then read what you've written and ask yourself, "Honestly, would I want to listen to myself?" I think you know the answer.

The upside is that by writing it down, you will (hopefully) have gotten it out of your system, so you won't be walking around with all of that negative energy. When you complain—about money, family, your body, whatever—the negativity begins to weigh on you like a ton of bricks. Who needs that? Worse, who wants to be in the company of a person stooped over under the weight of those bricks? Think about that the next time you are tempted to whine.

Whining is pure negative energy. Is that what you want to carry into the lives of the people around you? I certainly don't. On the contrary, I want people to light up when they see me, to get excited. "Hey, here comes Khloé!"

Bench Presses for Your Mind

I became mentally stronger in the same way I became physically stronger: I took little bites. One doesn't start out by saying, "I'm going to bench-press two hundred pounds by the end of the week." You slowly add weight over time. The changes are small and incremental, and you steadily make your way toward a place of optimum health.

This approach makes perfect sense, but for some crazy reason, people still struggle with it.

Take my brother Rob. I love him and he knows I love him, but he fell into a deep, dark place and couldn't find his way back. I've tried to help him, as has the entire family, but our efforts have largely been in vain. From time to time, though, he decides he's going to fix things his way, and he plunges in headfirst. Inevitably, it doesn't work.

Not long ago he took a cue from me and started working out. He came out of the starting gate like a Thoroughbred, and for two weeks he never lagged, but on the third week he decided he'd had enough. Working out was not his thing. It was a waste of time. He decided he couldn't change his ways. The truth is, he wanted too much too soon, and his unrealistic expectations totally short-circuited his efforts.

It does not matter how slowly you go as long as you do not stop.

—Confucius

I have another friend who became depressed and turned to food and gained thirty pounds in three months, which only made her feel worse. She decided to get into the best shape of her life and committed to losing the weight by summer, and she was seriously motivated for about two weeks, but the combination of exercise and diet became too much for her, and she quit and gained even more weight.

She was unrealistic and impatient. Instead of telling herself she was going to lose thirty pounds in three months, she should have made a commitment to getting healthier. That's a manageable goal. If you aim too high, you're going to give up on yourself, and nothing is worse than giving up on yourself. When you have no passion for your own life, other people won't be passionate about you either.

The key is to set reasonable goals and to move toward them at a reasonable speed, and it always goes back to the issue of motivation. We all know that it's tough to get motivated, just as we know that without motivation, we seldom make progress in any area of our lives.

That was certainly the case for my brother Rob. I was doing everything in my power to try to help him, and my entire family accused me of being an enabler. They even brought it up on the show, totally ambushing me, and I proceeded to defend myself by attacking them. I was the only one who was there for him, I said. They didn't care.

None of that was true, of course. They *all* cared. My mother was heartbroken. She was desperate to get him help, and professionals were brought in, but even then nothing changed.

Okay, one thing changed: I realized I was making life too easy for Rob. I'm a very nurturing person and I was constantly checking up on him, making sure he had the food he liked, seeing if he needed anything from the store, asking what I could do to make him more comfortable, whether I could cook him dinner, etc. Even when I was out of town, I had my assistant check in on him twice a day. My sisters said that I was babying him and that he'd never leave the house if I didn't let him fend for himself. I argued with them because it was an emotional issue, and emotion tends to cloud your thinking. But looking back, I now realize they were right. I even lent him my Range Rover. Kim said, "If he's driving a Range Rover, why would he be motivated to get a car of his own?" She was right on that point, too. So I took the Range Rover away, and my mom, who had been very vocal about everything I had been doing wrong, lent him one of her cars! She had been accusing me of enabling him, and she'd been right, and now she was doing the exact same thing. But she couldn't help it. This was her little boy.

Enabling starts as an attempt to be kind and helpful to someone, but it backfires because the person needs to be doing it for himself or herself. Good intentions, lousy results.

Rob still lives with me, and maybe I'm weak, but I'm not going to put my brother out on the street on the off chance that he will make an effort to change his life. If he starts making progress, I'll be his biggest cheerleader. And maybe from time to time I can point him in the right direction with a gentle suggestion. But beyond that, there's not much I can do. He will make changes in his life when he is able to motivate himself. And as much as I wish I could light that fire for him, I now see that the chances of that happening are slim to none.

Over the last couple of years I've learned a lot about how to change my life, how to improve it. I've also learned the hard way that it is impossible to change other people's lives if they aren't genuinely ready to improve their lives themselves. After I'd really taken control of my own life and made myself strong, I realized that you can't save other people and they can't save you. If you want to change your life, you have to do it yourself.

At the end of the day, it's not about other people saving us, but about saving ourselves. We all want someone to hold us when life gets hard. We want someone to dry our tears. We want someone on our team to help guide us through the tough moments. But in the end, though we can draw comfort from others, we need to pick ourselves up and dust ourselves off, then walk tall and save ourselves.

I think it's hard for most of us to see that, especially when people we love are struggling. But all you can do is say, "Hey, I know you have a lot of shit going on, and if you want my help, I'm here." But you are not responsible for the well-being of others, and if you don't learn to disengage, you will end up frustrated and unhappy. I see that with parents all the time. They are so hooked into their kids that every bump along the road affects them, and as a result, everyone is unhappy.

We all have to navigate our own way through life. The sooner we become aware of this, the sooner we will begin to make meaningful changes.

Friendship

One element necessary for a good life is friendship, and learning how to pick the right friends is very important. You'll go through trials and tribulations, and eventually you'll figure out who your real friends are. Those are the people you really need to hold on to. Everyone is going to screw up from time to time, and they all deserve second chances, but friendship is a two-way street. If you're always giving, giving, giving and getting nothing in return, you need to take a closer look at why.

A lot of times it's about money, because money and friendship is a tough combination, and if you have money, as I do, it sometimes gets in the way. Some people don't understand that money isn't just being handed to me, that I work for it, that my day starts at 5:00 a.m. and doesn't end until I collapse on my bed late at night, exhausted but fulfilled. So when a friend of mine sleeps till noon, wakes up with a champagne hangover, then decides once more *not* to look for a job and calls to tell me she can't pay the rent that month—well, it really pisses me off. "Did you try to get a job?" "Are you working on changing your life?" "Do you have to hit the bars every night?" "Is this really how you want to live?"

People like that eventually stop being my friends. How can they be my friends when they can't even be good to themselves?

Strangely enough, some of my so-called friends get irritated when I don't pay for everything. A person who expects me to pick up the tab every time we go out, just because I'm in a good financial place, doesn't have the right to call herself a friend. She can call herself *inconsiderate*. On the other hand, if I have a friend who is having money trouble but is making an honest effort to get her life in order, I'm not against helping her. On the contrary, I'm glad to do what I can. But people who don't try to better their own lives just don't get it. You've got to beat on a lot of doors before the right one opens. I'm glad to support my friends, but I refuse to support laziness.

I also get irritated when people are easily defeated. That happened once with one of my best friends, and it really tested our relationship. She used to have zero tolerance for frustration. One little thing would go wrong and she'd say, "My life is a shambles!" She had excuses for everything.

A real friend is one who walks in when the rest of the world walks out.

—Walter Winchell

At one point I sat her down and asked her what she wanted to do, and she said she thought she'd like to get into the news business, with an eye toward becoming an announcer. I reached out to some friends and set up all these meetings, and she never went to any of them. I felt like I was helping her get to where she wanted to be and she wasn't as persistent as she should've been.

Eventually, she decided to get therapy in order to figure out why she was constantly sabotaging herself, and she figured it out. Now she has a great job and loves it, and happens to be a great worker. But the best part is that working has really changed her life. Nowadays, when she gets up in the morning, she's like me—full of energy and excited about the day ahead, and happy because her life has direction.

More recently, she signed up at Equinox. She has the best body ever, without having to work out, but now she goes three times a week and loves it. She has even begun to cook for herself. She goes on YouTube, finds a healthy recipe, then runs out to the store, picks up the ingredients, and makes herself a nice meal. "I'm not happy when I don't have something to distract me," she told me recently. And I said, "That's the way it is for all of us. We need to be active and occupied. That's why they have that saying, "An idle mind is the devil's playground.'"

She and I have been close friends for sixteen years. We've always been really close and I really respect her for taking the initiative to elevate her life and be aware of her faults and improve herself. She's upbeat and purposeful and energized, the kind of friend you want to have around. Before, she was often depressed, defeated, and devoid of ambition. I'm glad I gave her a second chance and I am doubly glad that she was able to turn herself around.

Sometimes you can help a friend find the right path. You in turn will find yourself inspired by some of your good friends—how they live their lives, the choices they make, even just the way they are. You will also inspire people close to you.

Friends may come to you for advice. Don't hesitate to share what you've learned; just keep it short and sweet and don't turn it into a lecture. You never know how people are going to react, and there's always a chance you can help. Maybe that one word from you will be exactly what they needed to hear, and it will make an actual difference in their life.

Recently, for example, my brother came home and said he ran into an old friend of ours who told him I had saved his life. "What are you talking about?" I said. "I talked to him for maybe ten minutes!" Apparently, those ten minutes had been enough. Our friend had had a couple of serious brushes with the law, and at one point I bailed him out of jail. Afterward I sat him down and had a little talk with him. I had no idea my words had made such a big impression! The only thing I remember telling him is that I valued him more as a human being than he valued himself, and that I wished he could see himself through my eyes. I guess he looked and saw what I saw and liked it.

Here's the thing: I've always been a big believer in speaking my mind, and that's what I did in his case. In my experience, honesty resonates. So I always say, *Use your voice. Speak up. Say something.* It may not do any good, and it probably won't save a life, but honesty will not hurt a person if it comes from a loving place. On the other hand, if you're trying to help someone by *criticizing* him, that's probably not going to fly. Honesty can be harsh or loving and gentle. Which do you think is the better choice?

It's All About You

The funny thing is, when you're starting out in life—eighteen, nine-teen, twenty—you are usually pretty clueless about what you want to do with yourself. And that's okay. Nobody's asking you for hard answers. What's *not* okay is to do nothing. Your mind needs exercise, too. And it's not going to get it without a push. And really, it doesn't matter what you do, as long as you're engaged and productive. You want to be a dog walker, fine. You want to join a circus, great. The choices you make shouldn't frighten you, because they're just temporary, and you can chalk them up to experience. If you end up running a multimillion-dollar dog-walking business, that's cool, too. Just don't be afraid to try new things, and learn to stop worrying about where they will lead. And don't act like you're too good for a job. That guy running the movie studio started in the mailroom at the William Morris Agency.

Even more important, try to understand that *you are making changes in your life for you; that it's all about you.* It's not about making your parents happy or your friends happy or your strange Uncle Seymour happy; it's about *making your life work.*

That reminds me of something that happened with Lamar, a real eye-opening experience. He'd been invited to be part of the U.S. basketball team in the 2012 Olympics, and I was super excited for him. I knew they were going to win the gold. They had LeBron and Kobe on the team, and they were asking Lamar to join, and I was so proud of him. What a lineup! And I wanted him to go for a couple of reasons. Like most of us, Lamar does better with structure. More important, I felt he was getting close to the end of his career, and I wanted him to go out with a bang, with an Olympic gold medal under his belt. So I pushed and I kept pushing until finally one day Lamar said, "Khloé, you can't win it for me. I need to want to win it on my own. And I don't want it the way you want it." Something clicked. I knew he was right. I wanted it so badly that I would have played in his place. Although my wanting it for him came from a good place, it made no sense, and Lamar knew it made no sense. *He had to want it for himself.*

No one
saves us but
ourselves. No
one can and no
one may. We
ourselves must
walk the path.

—Buddha

That's what I'm talking about when I say that you can be there for friends and family—support them, nurture them, lend a hand when they lose their way—but real change has to come from within. Moral of the story? Work on yourself.

Seven Rules for Choosing the Right Friends

1. Look for people who will enrich your life. It's nice to hang out with friends who share your interests, but people with interests of their own will broaden your horizons. There's a whole world out there you know nothing about, and they can help you explore.

2. Look for people with qualities you admire. Kindness. Empathy. Generosity. A sense of humor. Qualities you hope to continue to develop in yourself.

3. Look for honesty above all else. A true friend will be honest, even when it hurts. And we all need friends who are willing to protect us from our own worst impulses.

4. Surround yourself with people who want you to succeed. This seems like a no-brainer, but not everyone has your best interests at heart. A true friend will listen when you talk about your hopes and dreams, and she will encourage you to pursue the right ones.

5. Look for people who are driven. People with energy fuel your own energy, and people without energy will drain you. Who'd you rather hang out with?

6. Look beyond the surface. Idle chat and gossip are always a good time, but real connections come from digging deep. Real friends have substance; real friends are a treasure in the truest sense of the word.

7. Don't look for perfection in others, and steer clear of people who expect perfection in you. Life is not about perfection. Life is about striving for perfection. Anyone who doesn't understand that doesn't deserve to be your friend.

Negative Energy

Here's a sad reality, and forgive me for stating the obvious: There is a lot of negativity in the world. For some crazy reason, lots of people seem to take pleasure in bringing others down. It happens to everyone, and it tends to be magnified when you're a bit of a public figure, like me. I hear negative things about me on the social media every day, and sometimes a dozen times a day, but I put my blinders on and keep moving forward. I've gotten so good at it that I feel really desensitized to that type of negativity. It doesn't affect me as much as it used to because it doesn't register with the same power.

People are entitled to their opinions, sure, but that doesn't mean I have to buy into them. There's always the temptation to reply to some of the nastier comments, but that's only going to fuel the negativity. People who post that kind of shit are either mean or stupid or both, and you don't need them in your life.

The trick is to develop enough confidence to listen to yourself and to trust your own opinions. In fact, I'd venture to say that your own opinion is the only one that really matters.

Strength of mind is in many ways more challenging that strength of body. There are a number of reasons for this, not the least of which is that we tend to be more negative than positive. And I'm not just talking about me. I've read many articles on the subject, and apparently our brains are wired for bad news because that's what helped us survive in the wild. When a caveman was out hunting, for example, he imagined a lion behind every rock, and nine times out of ten he was wrong. But when he did encounter the lion, he was ready for it, and that negative thinking saved his life.

Weird, isn't it? And I know it's true from personal experience. We gravitate toward the negative. If I'm having a great day, and nine people tell me I look good, I'm happy. But if the tenth person says I look tired, that's the comment that stays with me. One negative remark can ruin your whole day.

I have found that the most critical element in developing a strong mind is figuring out how to stay positive, and that's a challenge on a couple of major fronts.

The first relates to that little voice inside your head. Yeah, it's you again, talking to you. Being negative, usually. And boy, it's hard to shut that little voice up sometimes. And the stuff it's saying! You're not smart enough, you're not good enough, you'll never pull that off, and so on and so forth, nonstop—a sort of running negative commentary on your life. A friend told me that Buddhists call this our "monkey mind," because of the endless chatter and all the jumping around. That same friend told me to stop arguing with that voice and not to listen when it's being negative, which is most of the time, and little by little I'm getting better at it. That voice is just me trying to undermine myself, being a total Debbie Downer. It's my insecurity speaking, coupled with our natural human proclivity toward pessimism. So I've conditioned myself to stop listening when she's negative, though lately when she pisses me off, I've committed myself to proving her wrong. If Debbie Downer tells me my dinner party is going to be a disaster, I tell her, "Yeah? You just watch, bitch!" And that gives me all the motivation I need to make it a resounding success.

The result of this exercise has been to make me a stronger, more positive person. I bench-press away the negativity, hour after hour, day after day, and I'm building some awesome mental muscles.

On this issue of optimism, I've also learned a lot from Cici, who is a cousin of mine on my father's side. She's in her sixties and lives in Texas. Some years ago she was diagnosed with cancer, but to this day she is the most positive and beautiful human being I have ever met. She has infectious energy and an unbelievable outlook on life. Whenever I speak to her, she is so excited and attentive and vivacious that her energy comes through the phone. Her enthusiasm has made me understand what it means to truly appreciate life. If I tell her, "I bought these really cool Ralph Lauren drinking glasses," she says, "Oh my God! I'm in front of the computer. Tell me what they're called so I can Google them while we're on the phone." When I told her I was writing a book about being strong in body, mind, and heart, she said, "Oh my god! I can't wait. It's going to be a bestseller."

Once you replace negative thoughts with positive ones, you'll start having positive results.

—Willie Nelson

She has a heart of gold. She is honest at all times, but she does it in such an uplifting and supportive way that you love her for it, even when it stings a little. From Cici I've learned that it's not what you say, but how you say it.

She makes me look at life through different eyes and helps me understand that every minute counts. She makes me appreciate my own life, because she appreciates it, and because she knows every waking minute is a gift. Here she is, struggling with chemo treatments, losing her hair, being forced to think about the limited time she has left, and the irony is that she's the person I call when I'm down and need a little pep talk. Crazy, isn't it? I should be calling to try to brighten her day, but she invariably brightens mine.

So yeah, staying positive is critical. We could all learn a great deal from Cici. But most people never lose their ingrained negativity, which can be very bad for your mental health. You need to address that in yourself, and you need to steer clear of negative people.

Whenever Debbie Downer starts raining on my parade, I repeat a little mantra that always works for me: *The soul becomes dyed with the color of our thoughts and I want to paint my soul in vivid and bright colors.* Take it. It's yours. You can thank me later.

Let It Go

While we're on the topic of negative people, I need to point out that there's no point in trying to change or somehow "educate" them. That's an exercise in futility. People change only when they are ready to change, so don't waste your energy. I promise you, it's not going to happen. The one thing you can change, however, is the way you *respond* to them. As I get older, as I continue to work those mental muscles, I've learned that I don't have to react to every asshole on the planet.

There are two kinds of people in this world. One kind drops her iPhone, breaks it, and curses and stamps her feet like a spoiled child. The other one puts the phone back in her back pocket and adds an item to her to-do list: *Go to Apple Store*. Which would you rather be?

Say you're in traffic and somebody cuts you off. You can get upset and flip the offender the bird or pretend you're taking a picture of his license plate to send to the DMV, but that only makes things worse. It upsets *you*. You're like a kid having a temper tantrum, and the only person you're hurting is you. And honestly, it has nothing to do with you; he's the one with the problem. So I say again, *Let it go*.

I'm not saying it's easy. I remember one time Lamar and I were supposed to meet for a couples therapy session and he didn't show up. I kept thinking, "He must not be very invested in saving our marriage if he can't even show up for couples therapy!" I did the session without him, and when I left, I was so upset that I decided to work my feelings out at the gym. Except I'd forgotten how late it was and the gym was closed. I remember pulling into the parking lot and bursting into tears.

Later, when I finally reached Lamar, I asked him why he didn't show up. And you know what he said? "It's too hard." *It's too hard!* "It's hard for me, too!" I said. That experience opened my eyes. We're all dealing with our own shit. Everyone is going through stuff we can't even begin to imagine. That's why they do bad things. They hurt us with their own pain. You have to learn to accept other people's frailties. You have to remember that it's usually about them, seldom about you.

Still, the list of things that can set us off is endless. Someone doesn't return your phone call or arrives late for dinner. Or the store is out of almond milk. These are insignificant experiences that have absolutely nothing to do with you, and yet they end up darkening your day. But only because you let them.

You know what I do when that happens to me? I ask myself, "Why am I getting so pissed? How does my reaction really help this situation?" And I already know the answer. I'm getting pissed because I'm making this personal, and my reaction is only making things worse. Sometimes the simple act of posing those questions is enough to defuse the situation and help me get back on track.

Author Richard Carlson points out that your life, like a car, is driven from the inside—that you need to be in control. He also thinks you would do well to enjoy the journey and worry less about the destination. "As you focus more on becoming more peaceful with where you are, rather than focusing on where you would rather be, you begin to find peace right now, in the present," he writes in *Don't Sweat the Small Stuff* . . . "Then, as you move around, try new things, and meet new people, you carry that sense of inner peace with you. It's absolutely true that, 'Wherever you go, there you are.'"

All of this takes work, of course. I'm not Gandhi. But looking back I know I'm making progress. For example, when I was about twelve and was attending private school in Los Angeles, one of the new teachers couldn't believe that Kim and Kourtney were my sisters. "You're really related to those girls?" she asked, incredulous. And I kept saying, "*Yes*, they're my sisters." "Same set of parents?" "Yes!"

I couldn't understand why she was questioning it. It didn't fully register at the time, but later, when I thought about it, I found it incredibly hurtful. She might as well have said, "Those two are in another league. You got left behind." Were my sisters really so much more beautiful than me?

This experience was hurtful and damaging, and it stayed with me for a very long time, and I'm sure it contributed to my teenage insecurities. But if I knew then what I know now, I wouldn't have let it affect me in the same way. I would have let it go.

Still, you can't ignore the power others have over you, the way they can affect you to the very core. You want an even crazier example? During my marriage, according to the media, I was pregnant at least eight times. At one point, my own publicist called to ask me if the rumors were true, saying that a nurse in my doctor's office had apparently confirmed it. I denied it. Vehemently. But suddenly I began to wonder, and I was filled with self-doubt. I went to CVS to get a pregnancy kit just to be sure I wasn't pregnant. My husband looked at me in disbelief, realizing that this was a whole new level of crazy. "Girl, what are you talking about?" he said. "We both know you're not pregnant!" I knew, of course, but all those screeching voices had filled me with doubt, and I could no longer hear my logical self.

I actually did pick up a pregnancy kit, and of course the results were negative, but the fact that I had been driven to that extreme was frightening.

This is what I'm talking about when I say that you can't let other people define you and affect you with their talk. That crazy pregnancy business—that would never happen today. It wasn't even three years ago, but I've made huge strides since and I feel myself getting mentally stronger all the time. People are always going to talk shit about you, especially if you are in the public eye, and some of them will take pleasure in tearing you down, and at times it will hurt, but you work through it and get strong.

You have to know yourself, believe in yourself, and define your own self.

Easy, huh?
Well, no.

Getting Through the Bad Days

I have bad days, too, and I've learned to deal with them. Even little things help. For example, no matter how horrible I'm feeling, I get out of bed. Literally wallowing in misery is not the answer. Next, brush your teeth and take a shower. It makes a huge difference. It means you're getting ready for the day. Now walk into that kitchen and drink your tall glass of water and make your coffee and get going. If you have nowhere to go, take a walk or go for a hike; even a drive can help. Get out of your cocoon. Shake things up. And for god's sake, stop feeling sorry for yourself.

Self-pity is the worst. I often deal with it by turning to music. Music is a great mood shifter. I'm not someone who cries a lot, and certainly not in front of other people, but from time to time I get just as sad as the next person. I can go to a three-hankie movie with you and not shed a tear, but the minute I walk through my front door, I fall apart. If the sadness stays with me, I'll get back in my car and drive around aimlessly and sing along to Sam Smith. I'm not a good singer, but it still helps.

I find music amazingly therapeutic. (It has actually been shown to reduce stress!) Sometimes I'll even listen to sad music, because it makes me feel connected to the sadness in the world and makes me feel less alone. But a moment later I'll put on Beyoncé, turn the music up *loud*, and—if the spirit moves me—dance my way into a better mood. (No wonder there's a whole field of music therapy! It really works!)

The other option is mindless television. I like murder mysteries,

Problems are not stop signs, they are guidelines.

—Robert H. Schuller

especially those crazy stories on *Dateline* and *20/20*. When I'm watching those shows, I forget about myself and my little problems, at least for the duration. The downside is that the creepy shows stay with me, so to shake those icky feelings, I have to switch to something fun, like reruns of *Friends* or *Sex and the City*.

On some level, music and TV can be a form of escape, and I'm aware of that. But I don't see that as a bad thing. I believe we all need to escape from our reality from time to time. Maybe that's what keeps us sane. There's a reason people are given paid vacations and are forced to take them! We need a refuge. For me, taking a break from a problem and coming back to it when I'm in a calmer, better place can help me deal with it much more effectively. Nothing gets resolved when emotions are running high, which is why I've learned to wait until the storm has passed. (Don't make a permanent decision when you're in the grip of a temporary emotion!) When I'm calm, life becomes infinitely more manageable. And when we begin to manage our lives, we become stronger, better people.

The Art of Journaling

I love journaling. If something specific is troubling me, I'll often try to work it out at my desk or on the computer screen. It's like having a conversation with myself. I find analyzing the problem by writing about it immensely therapeutic. It's especially helpful because I'm less "shary" than my sisters, probably because I don't want everything to be about me, me, me, and when I'm journaling I give myself permission to be self-absorbed. I don't think there's anything wrong with a little self-absorption from time to time, especially if the goal is to make yourself a better person.

Journaling is a great way to literally get things out of your system. When you see the words in front of you, the issue becomes somehow more manageable. I also see writing as a concentrated form of thinking. It's just you and your thoughts and feelings, working things out with yourself. It's like, "Okay! I understand that now. Putting it into words has really made things clearer. Now I can work on getting it out of my system."

And even when there's nothing specific on my mind, journaling is a good exercise. I might just think of a single word—*love, flowers, passion*, for example—and write it out by hand. And then I'll consider absolutely everything that this word means to me. This exercise takes me to some interesting places.

But probably the most valuable lesson I've learned from journaling is that we are never fully in control of our emotions. Life is uncertain, and uncertainty can be scary; to expect otherwise is only going to make you crazy. You're not running the show, trust me, and when you think you are, remember the Serenity Prayer:

God, grant me the serenity to accept the things
 I cannot change,
The courage to change the things I can
And the wisdom to know the difference.

Sometimes the act of writing about the things I can't control makes me feel more in control. And sometimes I feel in control because I know I have no control. I know this line doesn't seem to make sense, but read it again and you'll get it.

The other great thing about journaling is that you can use it to review your day. You look back on the things that went right and those that went wrong, and you spend a few minutes thinking about the way you handled various situations. When I started doing this, I realized that I have a tendency to focus on my mistakes, and then I'd obsess and feel bad all over again. I'd think about what I could have done differently and where I went wrong, and I didn't like the feeling. But then I realized that I could learn from those mistakes, that each mistake was a teachable moment, so instead of beating myself up, I'd try to figure out how I could handle things if and when I found myself in a similar situation. In that light, journaling became an even more positive experience. My mistakes were all about learning, not about self-criticism, and I knew I could do better. My mistakes were making me stronger.

And speaking of self-criticism, I'll say this: There's a place for it in all of our lives, because it's important to acknowledge your flaws, but don't overdo it. In other words, deal with your shortcomings and own up to your mistakes, but don't beat yourself up. Here again, journaling has proved immensely helpful. When you start attacking yourself on the page, you'll see it right away, and you'll stop doing it. Why be unkind to yourself? There's more than enough unkindness to go around, so why punish yourself by adding to it?

My only negative experience with journaling happened a couple of years ago, and it has nothing to do with the act itself: One of my journals went missing. I don't believe it was filled with any earth-shattering revelations, and I'm certainly not obsessing about it, but as a result I became very cautious. I worry about it happening again, so now I destroy my journals as soon as I'm done writing. I shred the handwritten pages and I even delete the files on my computer. That may seem a little excessive, especially for someone whose entire life seems to be documented on TV and by the press, but it makes me feel safer.

I will never give up journaling, however. To me, it has been the most effective way of facing my demons, and I'm a big believer in confronting those demons head-on. If you don't try to deal with your problems, they're going to come back and bite you in the ass. And the more you ignore them, the stronger they get. The only way to defeat your demons is to identify them and to begin to address the underlying problem. "Okay, that's my insecurity talking." "Okay, that's jealousy." "Okay, that's loneliness." At that point you can get to work on it. And it *is* work. You're working your emotional muscles. You're trying to get strong.

You also have to be realistic. The demons never go away, and they will test you, but you will get better at keeping them at bay. And I see real beauty in that. Life isn't about perfection, but about growth. And when I do battle with those demons, even if at times I find myself bruised and battered, I know I'm getting stronger. People with the worst scars have the best stories. In order to grow as people, we often have to go to war with dark parts of ourselves; that's what positive change is all about.

And the work never ends. I know there are plenty of demons inside me I haven't even met, but I'm preparing for them.

When my father died, for example, I met my Really Angry Demon. I was so angry, I was practically breathing fury at that point. My rage was so extreme that I lashed out at everyone. If somebody tried to say anything even mildly comforting, I had to fight the urge to snarl (and I usually lost). That's how my sorrow manifested itself, as rage. That demon breathed fire.

Even now, looking back on it, I'm embarrassed by what a bitch I was. But at age nineteen I didn't have the tools to deal with the pain. At age nineteen I didn't realize that life shows everyone its claws. If I had simply found the strength to go down into the darkness, to sit alone with my loss and my sadness, that would not have happened.

Facing the Pain

Sometimes, despite our best efforts, we find ourselves in a dark, lonely place, and we need help. My friend Malika, for example, will call me out of the blue and say, "Can we do a wine night?" She comes over, I crack a bottle of wine, and I listen to her talk while I'm organizing my closets (because I'm *always* organizing my closets). By the time she feels better about whatever was weighing on her mind, I feel great, too, because my closets look marvelous.

I have other friends who meet for a girls' lunch once a month, and they share absolutely everything that's on their minds. That's not my thing, because I'm more self-nurturing and private, but it works for them and it could work for you.

I also think therapy is great. I think it's healthy to admit that you need help with certain problems, because that's a first step toward a solution.

Toward the end of my marriage, things began to get unbearably painful. I didn't reach the levels of misdirected anger that I'd experienced after my father died, but I was in a very bad place, and he was in a worse place, and we both realized that we weren't going to get anywhere by holding hands and singing "Kumbaya." So we went to couples counseling, and we finally began to come to terms with the fact that the marriage was pretty much over. I was truly heartbroken. When I first got married, I felt as if I was really coming into my own as a person. Being a wife completed me. I know it sounds corny, but I loved the whole experience—falling in love, getting engaged, making a home, taking care of my man, taking care of his kids, etc. Maybe those emotions seem a bit old-fashioned, but they were true at the time and they continue to be my values to this very day. So yeah, watching my marriage come crashing down was the absolute worst.

When it ended, when Lamar left, when it was truly over, things didn't get any easier. When I got married, I was no longer simply one of the Kardashians; I had my own life and a separate identity. I had broken free. I was an adult (finally). In sharing my life with Lamar, I felt as if my entire world had become greatly enriched. But with Lamar gone, it was as if I had taken a giant backward step. I was back to being Khloé, but a somewhat more "damaged" version. And as much as I loved my family, losing Lamar had left me horribly adrift.

Then one night, during one of my darker moments, I remembered a conversation I'd had with my father many years earlier, when I was maybe thirteen or fourteen, about that teacher who had compared me unfavorably to my sisters. "She made me feel like I'm not even part of this family," I told my father. "She made me feel ugly." And my father wiped away my tears and said, "Let me tell you something, Khloé. You've always had to fight a little harder than your sisters for everything, and as a result you are much stronger than either of them. In fact, you're the only one I'm *not* worried

about. You have more inner strength than you can imagine, and I promise you this: You are always going to land on your feet."

Remembering that conversation helped me survive the end of my marriage. I realized I *was* strong. I still had plenty of work to do on myself, but I knew I was going to get there.

Life Is About Second Chances

During this time, I often went to see Pastor Brad, one of the few people I have always turned to in times of need, one of the few people I can really talk to. Pastor Brad is a family friend, going back to when my parents were together, and he was also the man who married Lamar and me.

Pastor Brad is still a huge part of my life. Unlike most of the rest of my family, most of whom are practicing Christians, I don't go to church every Sunday, but I still see him privately from time to time to talk about my issues. All of us can use a helping hand occasionally, and Pastor Brad has been mine.

One of the great things I've learned from him is that life is all about second chances. No matter how badly you screw up, you can start fresh the very next minute. But you have to have the drive to do it.

The other thing I learned from him is that perfection is unattainable. Our brains are wired to want more and to never be satisfied, so we're never going to win that battle, but that doesn't mean we shouldn't *strive* for perfection. Some people are perfectly happy with who they are and how they look and how they behave, and that's fine, but I never want to stop growing and improving and trying in every way to better myself. But I'm doing it for me, to make *myself* happy, and I think it's important to define what perfection means to you.

I also think it's important to be honest with yourself about the areas where you are coming up short, because denying your flaws is the best way to let them rule you. Here again, though, you have to be your own judge. And you have to decide what you want to work on. Don't listen to other people. These decisions are between you and you. But don't bullshit yourself about what you see in the mirror. If you don't like it, you can change it. My feeling is that as long as you're making progress as a human being—becoming a slightly better version of yourself, one day at a time—that's already a form of perfection.

There's an old joke that's really only half a joke: "If you want to make God laugh, tell him your plans." Life is full of unexpected twists

Our greatest weakness lies in giving up. The most certain way to succeed is always to try just one more time.

—Thomas A. Edison

and turns, which is pretty obvious, but most of us have a hard time accepting that.

When I went to see Pastor Brad, still hurting over the end of my marriage, he helped me understand that everything happens for a reason. When we're in the thick of it, though—my father's death, my divorce—we're mostly angry or in pain, and it's hard to believe that someday we'll look back and see the situation in a larger context.

When my father died, I questioned God. "Why did you take him from me? What were you thinking? What did I do to anger you?" Later, after the anger and the drinking, and after Kourtney set me up in the new store, I realized that other forces were at play. I didn't have my father anymore, but I knew I would survive the loss.

As Pastor Brad put it, we all lose people we love, and we all suffer pain and heartbreak, but we get through it and new good things do happen.

Pastor Brad had gone though his own personal challenges. His marriage fell apart, and he too got a divorce, and his parish responded by kicking him out. When my mother first told me that story, I was horrified. The church—aren't they supposed to be the good guys? How could they do that to one of their own, especially in a time of need? I was always taught about forgiveness, but the very people who were teaching the community about love, forgiveness, and not being judgmental were doing the opposite.

He ended up working at a local Starbucks. He slowly found his way back, and now he has a church of his own. So he did get through it, and good things did happen. But only because he didn't wallow in misery or anger; instead he dusted himself off and picked himself up and began to move forward. I'm still pissed at the church on his behalf, because I think they behaved abominably, but I am also really impressed with Pastor Brad, and with the way he made a commitment to rebuilding his life. The secret is really simple: *You fall down, you get up*.

So yes, my marriage was over. And it hurt like hell. And I wallowed, *briefly*, and when I'd had enough self-pity I put one foot in front of the other and kept moving. That's what strength of mind is all about. You get up and power forward. You become your own engine. You *motor* your way through that day and the next one and the one after that. And every day gets a little easier. Well, usually. We all have days that feel like total hell (and they pass, too).

Vulnerability Is *Not* a Sign of Weakness

Thinking back, I realize that one of the most important things I learned from Pastor Brad is that I had to continue to allow myself to be vulnerable. When people get hurt, they often shut down, and it makes perfect sense: Who enjoys getting hurt? But it's the wrong way to go. To be alive is to be vulnerable, and sometimes we don't see that. In fact, lots of people—men and women alike—see vulnerability as a sign of weakness. But without risk, there are no rewards. Knowing this, I am always genuine. I don't have any trouble telling others that I miss them or that I love them, even if I risk not hearing the same thing back. If I don't tell them what's in my heart, I am being dishonest, and I'd rather be vulnerable than dishonest. I'm not trying to be cool, I'm trying to be genuine, and I want at all times to be true to my feelings.

And never, ever tell someone you love him or her just because you want to hear that back. That's a terrible idea. That's like buying someone a present because your birthday is around the corner and you want to remind him or her to get you something nice. You don't give to receive. You give from the heart. And honest words are a gift from the heart.

The other day one of my girlfriends said, "Last night, I told Paul I loved him, and you know what the bastard said? He said, 'I know.'"

I thought that was a real dick thing to do, but I also told my girlfriend that she had no right to be pissed. She had told him she loved him only because she wanted to hear him say it back. It didn't come from the heart, and in fact she wasn't even sure she loved him. She was testing him because she was worried about getting too deeply involved and getting hurt. That's no way to live your life. Taking emotional risks is scary, sure, but the thought of living without risk should scare you more.

I know this from personal experience. I always tried to be a really tough girl. I had feelings and wouldn't acknowledge them, and my life changed for the better when I finally allowed myself to be vulnerable. To close your heart might protect you, but it's not really living. And trust me, if you get hurt, it's not the end of the world.

I know I'm different, and I embrace it. I'm a little old school, absolutely. I don't have a problem being submissive to a man—and by submissive I mean cooking his meals, loving him up, and taking care of him emotionally. I don't think that makes me weak. On the contrary, it shows that I'm strong enough and secure enough to be exactly who I am.

Mostly, though, I like the fact that I'm honest with myself and with the people around me. I don't play games anymore, and it makes me crazy when I see my girlfriends doing it. "Hello! Grow up! We're not children anymore!"

The Art of Romance

I have one friend who is a hopeless romantic. She'll meet a guy and ask me how many days she should wait before calling him. I tell her

I don't get it. If you feel like calling a guy, call him. Or a guy will text her and she'll say, "I have to wait twenty minutes before I text him back." And I'm shocked. "Why? Who made up that stupid rule? When I get a text, if my phone is next to me, I'll text back right away, if not sooner. How does that reflect badly on me? How does that make me *weak*?"

She doesn't seem to understand that game playing is a sign of weakness. If you have to play games, you're obviously not secure enough to be yourself.

The other thing that makes me crazy is the way some women expect their husbands or boyfriends to read their minds. One of them will say, "I don't want to tell Chad that I want to go to Santa Barbara next weekend. It's our one-year anniversary, and he should be able to figure it out, because that's where we spent our first weekend together." I think that's crazy. For one thing, you are setting yourself up for disappointment. What if he doesn't figure it out on his own? Does that make him a bad person? Of course not! And why do you need him to be a mind reader? Wouldn't it be a lot simpler to say, "Chad, why don't we go to Santa Barbara this weekend, to the same hotel we went to after we got together?" That would be the exact right way to do it, but some women like to complicate their lives.

And that's certainly not the way I do things. I think communication is critical in every relationship, and I'm big on clarity. Say what you mean and mean what you say. Don't be afraid to ask for a hug if you need a hug. For me, communicating is about putting your cards on the table. I want people to see my cards. And if I need something from them, I will tell them.

And it's funny, because I got a call from one of my girlfriends while I was working on this section of the book. She had just met a guy who is 100 percent Armenian, and she's not even part Armenian, and she's worried because she really likes him, but she knows that many Armenians will not date outside their culture. If she was twenty years old, she wouldn't care, but she is thirty and is sufficiently interested in him to hope that the relationship goes to a good place, but she doesn't know what to do.

So I said to her, "Why not just be honest with him? Ask him if he thinks you have a future together. It's a legitimate question, and it's also a way of letting him know that you have feelings for him."

I don't know how that's going to turn out, and I don't believe she has said anything to him *yet*, but even if the guy ends up running for the hills I believe it is the right thing to do. This is about *her* feelings and *her* life, and I don't think she should invest the next two years into a guy who might then turn around and tell her that he can't marry her because she's not Armenian. If she broaches it now and it ends, she'll be doing herself a favor. How would she feel if she invested two years in a guy who never had any intention of marrying her anyway?

Better to deal with the pain now, today, than to have to deal with it two years from now, when it will be a hundred times worse. And I'm not saying that's going to happen! I sure hope it doesn't—I hope this Armenian turns out to be the man of her dreams—but I'm just saying it *might*. And you know what? It could happen anyway, because she can't control his honesty, but she can certainly control her own.

There's nothing wrong with wanting to know where you stand in a relationship. Every relationship involves risk and uncertainty, but you can minimize it with honesty. Honesty is a good way to put your cards on the table and to look out for yourself. And if you aren't looking out for yourself, who is?

Brad Johnson

Pastor
California Community Church
Agoura Hills, CA

Whenever you make a bad choice in life, whenever you look back with regret, it's important to remember that life is about second chances. From a perspective of faith, I believe the message of Christ is that anybody can have a fresh start. God specializes in second chances, which is a foundational principle of the Christian faith: Nobody is ever finished, the story is never over. I really, truly believe that.

Unfortunately, people tend to get stuck in their former chapters. "Oh, that was a crappy part of my life." "That was a part I'm sad about." "That chapter's where I got hurt." They fundamentally cannot move forward because they keep rereading past chapters, and it keeps them from writing new chapters. And when you're busy living in the past, the present is going to pass you by.

Everyone has pain. Everyone struggles. We all make bad choices, we all have regrets, and we all suffer. But things change. It is inevitable. The pain will lessen in due course, often sooner than you can imagine. And while it's both healthy and appropriate to grieve, to sit quietly with your pain or anger, it's just as important to let go—to move forward into the future.

Just make sure you learn from those experiences. Somebody once said, "If you make a mistake, you can only do it once, because if you do the same thing again it's no longer a mistake; it's a choice."

I have made my share of mistakes and more. When I was a pastor, for example, I was unfaithful to my wife and I lost my marriage and my ministry. I hurt a lot of people and felt horrible, and I decided to quietly disappear. I did not want to be in the ministry again—I didn't think I deserved it—and I didn't want to be in the public eye again.

For a time, I thought I was destined to spend the rest of my life wallowing in shame and guilt. I fell into a deep depression. I went from a solid middle-class life to the verge of homelessness. Then I landed a job making $8.25 at Starbucks and was thrilled by the opportunity. I brought a good attitude to the job and began to feel productive again, and that led to other part-time jobs. Slowly, one step at a time, I began to find my way back. That was the key: to be positive, to be hopeful. Not to wallow in and become destroyed by regret, but to accept with gratitude the small miracles that came my way.

While I was in the process or rebuilding my life, I got a call from Khloé's mother, Kris Kardashian. She told me that she felt God was leading her to open a church in her area of California, a church that was redemptive and believed in forgiveness and grace and second chances, and that—knowing my story—she felt I would be the best person to lead that church.

I saw that phone call from Kris as a sign of God's love. He wanted me to know that I had not been abandoned, and that there were people out there who still believed in me and were ready to lead me out of the valley and back into the light.

I was very moved. One of the most important lessons I took from the experience is that anyone who has been to a dark and difficult place has to learn to reach out to people who are struggling with their own challenges. It is our responsibility to help others find their way through the tough times. That is the foundation of compassion. The world is full of flawed people, and not all of them have your best interests at heart, but it's important to approach everyone with love. It's easy to be jaded and cynical, but that's a hard way to live. It's better to give people the benefit of the doubt, to take another chance on relationships and on love. It'll make you a little more vulnerable, certainly, but it will open you up to a richer, fuller life.

In every life, there is struggle. No one is immune from pain and suffering. But it won't last. Life moves forward. The circumstances will change. This applies to both the bad feelings and the good. Nothing lasts forever. When you think about this, the only moment you really have is the present, and you have to learn to enjoy it. This is what people mean when they talk about *living in the now*. You take the lessons you've learned from the past, both good and bad, and you move forward. But don't be in too much of a hurry. At the end of the day, all you really have is the present moment. If you can learn to live without regret about the past, and without too much anxiety about the future, you will begin to truly live.

As I said earlier, we all encounter defeats, but we must never be defeated. Every day is a clean page; every day is another opportunity to write a new story. It's your story. Write the story you want to live.

Nothing Lasts Forever

My mother went through her own version of hell, and I hope she doesn't mind that I use her as an example. When I was too young to know what was going on, O. J. Simpson was charged with murdering Nicole Brown Simpson and Ronald Goldman. It was billed as the Trial of the Century, and my mother had a very personal stake in it: Nicole had been her best friend.

Now imagine how she felt when my father, Robert Kardashian, became a member of the dream team that defended O.J. and got him acquitted. He basically helped the man who she believed had murdered her best friend. My parents were no longer married at the time, but my mother went to court almost every day, and she sat there watching her ex-husband trying to save the life of the man who had allegedly murdered Nicole. I am sure that she thought she would never get beyond it, but she did. Less than a year after the trial ended, my parents became close again. My father would often join us for dinner at least once a week, was always there for Thanksgiving and Christmas and birthdays, and regularly played golf with Bruce. After all, they had three daughters and a son to raise, and they had to get beyond the pain and anger for the sake of the family.

Looking back on that story reminds me of another conversation I had with Pastor Brad. People say, "Nothing lasts forever," and it's true. But it's not as sad as it sounds. When good things fall apart, we're unhappy and angry and resentful. It's like we want to look up at the sky and shake a fist at God. But what we lose sight of is that *unhappy* situations don't last either. So when you're in the middle of a breakup or a deep depression, or you feel bad because you got passed over for a promotion, you need to remind yourself that things *are going to get better*. And that's not bullshit. It's the absolute truth. Life moves on, one way or another, and everything changes. The good things don't last, but the bad things don't last either.

I'll say it again: Nothing lasts forever. Take the Academy Awards, for example. I've often wondered what it's like for those amazing actresses. You hear your name called and you get up there in front of a billion people, probably with tears in your eyes, and someone hands you your Oscar. In your heart you probably already know that this is never going to happen again (unless you're Meryl Streep); that this is the pinnacle, that this is as good as it's ever going to get, and that in some ways it's all downhill from here. But that's the way life works. Ebb and flow. Up and down. Yin and yang. And if there isn't another Oscar in your future, there will be other things that will be joyous and exciting in their own way. Not in front of a billion people, obviously, but maybe in front of the people who really matter to you.

To be strong of mind is to understand and to accept that. And to get to a place where you can accept that, well—just open your eyes. This is the way the world works, a law of nature: *Nothing lasts forever.* You cannot change that through force of will, and you certainly can't change it through magical thinking. Accept this and you're ahead of the game. When something good comes to an end, you won't be crushed. And when you run into some unpleasantness, you know it's not going to last. Life is a roller-coaster ride, sure, but if you understand this, you'll learn to handle the ups and downs.

Whenever I read a memoir, I am always fascinated by what people went through to succeed. Half the time you can't believe they survived! It teaches you that the people who make it are the ones who hang on, even when the storm is at its worst.

I'll always remember that line from Bette Davis as Margo

Channing in *All About Eve*: "Fasten your seat belts. It's going to be a bumpy night."

Bumpy, yes—but that doesn't necessarily mean it won't be fun.

Looking back, and knowing that I still have a lot of work to do on myself, I can honestly say that I feel pretty good about some of the things I've managed to change. One thing, for example, is that I've always been honest, sometimes brutally so, and even though it comes from a good place I realize that I can come off as pretty harsh. Well, I'm working on that, and I've been more careful about my delivery and my choice of words. I've noticed the change in me and I hope the people closest to me have noticed it, too.

I'm also trying to be more patient. Most of my life I've been one of those people who doesn't think instant gratification is fast enough, and that's not a great way to live. Lately, with great effort, I'd like to think I'm getting a little better at it, but I'm still pretty damn impatient and I know I have a long way to go. Doesn't mean I'm going to stop working on it, though.

I'm still working on getting stronger, too. Physically, emotionally, spiritually. But that's sort of the point of life, right? When you're not working on that, you're not living.

It's all about awareness, even self-awareness, which brings us to the big topic du jour, mindfulness. I talked a little about this earlier, about that negative voice in your head that keeps undermining your self-confidence, but this goes a little deeper. This is about trying *to be present in every moment of your life*, which—not to put too fine a point on it—is probably one of the most challenging things ever.

I'm working on it, though, and I'm going to keep working on it until I get it right. We live in the age of distraction, and many of our most precious moments pass us by. We're either thinking about what's next, living in the future, or obsessing about something that happened earlier in the day or week, living in the past. And the result is that the present goes by without your having been there for it. The past you can't change; learn from it and move on. As for the future, if you're always thinking about what's next you'll still be thinking about what's next when you get to where you thought you wanted to be, and suddenly the thing you were looking forward to with such eagerness is gone, too. In short, your inability to be present is making you miss out on your own life.

In an effort to address this, I've tried a few things that are beginning to prove helpful. First, I try not to multitask when I'm with family and friends. (This doesn't count at work, where multitasking is a *necessity!*) If I'm having lunch, I try to focus on lunch, and I do my best to ignore my phone. My aunt Shelli has a rule about no phones at the dinner table, and I think this is definitely the way to go. When I'm driving, I'm really driving, and my only distraction is listening to music. (Researchers at Cohen Children's Medical Center in New Hyde Park found that among teenagers there are now more fatal accidents from texting and driving than from drinking and driving, so don't even *think* about your phone.) When I'm with a friend, I try to really, truly listen, to be fully present, and if my monkey mind starts jumping around, I focus even harder. I call this *active listening*, and it really works.

Why does living in the moment make people happier? Because most of our negative thoughts are linked to the past or the future. As Mark Twain said, "I have known a great many troubles, but most of them never happened." What did he mean by that? That he spent altogether too much time obsessing about things that *might* happen, when in fact he could have let go of that simply by living in the present.

A lot of noise in life is just that, noise, and you have to figure out which noises you should be listening to. Otherwise you will move from one thing to the next without really appreciating *any* of it. If you are only half present, life doesn't register in a deep or meaningful way. And who wants to live half a life?

Here's the way I look at it. The past is gone, and the future is going to get here without your help. And unless you learn to be present in the moment, you're going to miss out on the best life has to offer. Make an effort to be fully present. Your life is richer than you think.

Part 3

HEART

Chapter 5
Be Mindful

A couple of years ago, I was sitting at home one night, flipping through the channels for something to watch, and stumbled across a recent rerun of *KUWTK*. In the show, I was having a heated exchange with my mother, and I was shocked by the way I was addressing her. I remember thinking, "Ugh, if that was my kid, I'd smack her."

Another time we got into a fight over a radio interview she'd arranged on my behalf. I told her that I wasn't interested in doing press with anyone who wanted to talk to me about Lamar, and she said I didn't have to worry because she had prescreened all the questions. "It'll be easy. Have fun." The interview went pretty well, but toward the end I got bombarded with questions about Lamar and kept my cool. Later, however, I took it out on my mother. "Mom, what the fuck is your problem? I told you I didn't want to talk about Lamar!" I don't even know why I was blaming her, but it was an ugly, thoughtless thing to do. The person who interviewed me had never shown her those questions—interviewers do that all the time—and I was wrong to blame her, especially in that ugly manner. She was gracious enough to accept my apology.

In some ways, this was the beginning of my journey toward greater mindfulness.

The Problem Is *You*

As upsetting as this incident was, however, for both my mother and me, I learned an important lesson: *I was the problem. My reaction was the problem.*

I spend an inordinate amount of time with my mother. Not only are we on the show together, but she is my manager. The truth is, sometimes I still speak to her in a harsh and unpleasant manner. After seeing those episodes, I tried to change my ways, to soften my exchanges with her, and I'd like to think I've had some success. I'm not there yet, but I'm trying, and I'm going to keep trying till I get it right.

I believe that what we put out in the world—our energy, our treatment of others, our work—is hugely important and has real effect. I also think that many of us aren't sufficiently aware of the way we behave with other people. I was lucky because the camera showed me something about myself that I desperately needed to address, and I've been working on it ever since.

Now I smile more often. I'm friendlier and more open. I take the time to notice little changes in the people around me: I tell them I like their hair or their new shoes or their beautiful smile. It really boils down to kindness, and one of the things I've learned about kindness is that it helps me as much as (maybe more than) it benefits the person I am kind to. When I'm kind, I feel good about myself. And I like to feel good about myself, so I try to practice

If you don't
like something,
change it.
If you can't
change it,
change your
attitude.

—Maya Angelou

kindness every day. Being kind is transformative: It affects everything that follows the act of kindness, and generally for the better!

Sometimes I fail. Sometimes I'm a total bitch. But I do my best to catch myself and get back on the kindness track. And like everything else in life, it takes practice. But it's not that hard. Really! You just need to become aware of how you treat other people. If you're not putting positive energy into the world, you're doing something wrong.

I was at a restaurant recently with a group of friends, and our waitress was so upbeat and happy that she put all of us into a great mood. So I'm not talking only about the way you treat your friends, but about the way you approach *everyone*. Even a simple smile can change the course of someone's day for the better. I want to be known for putting people in a good mood. I know I'm not always going to succeed—sometimes I get caught up in my own shit—but I am certainly going to try.

The Power of Kindness

A small act of kindness has terrific power. And if you do it often enough, it becomes second nature. You're working your kindness muscle. You're getting strong in ways you never even imagined.

When I was a kid, the whole family would be at the dinner table, and my father would always try to get us to talk about our day. Since he didn't really know my classmates and could seldom keep their names straight anyway, I would describe them through their looks. If I described a friend as "the brunette girl," that was fine with him. But if I spoke of "the girl with acne" or "the overweight girl," it would bother him. "Is that really the best way to describe her?" he would say.

Life's most
persistent
and urgent
question is,
"What are
you doing for
others?"

—Martin Luther King Jr.

He made me aware of the way I viewed other people. If it didn't come from a kind place, he wanted me to address that. It is easy to describe people through their flaws or imperfections, but my father taught me to try to find the positive in those around me. From him, I learned that you can find something to like in almost everyone, and that the right way to live is to focus on the *good* in people.

"What's another way to describe her?" he would say.

And I would say, "Well, she tells very funny stories."

And my father would say, "That's good. Now I'll always remember her as the girl who tells funny stories."

This lesson has stayed with me throughout my life: If you look for something positive in people, you will find it. And while it's human nature to judge others, you can teach yourself to judge from a place of generosity. Everyone struggles. Everyone has issues. Everyone is trying to figure out this business of living. If you look at it that way, it's easier to cut people a break when they behave badly.

Every day before work, my father would read the Bible, and he would often jot down the verses that spoke to him in a profound way. He would write the verses in his own hand on a three-by-five card; eventually he created a collection of cards, which piled up in a drawer. Some years ago, my sisters and I were brainstorming about what to get our brother, Rob, for his birthday, and we ended up creating this beautiful plaque filled with my father's handwritten quotes from the Bible. I know Rob was really moved by the gift, and he cherishes it to this day.

Another reminder of the power of kindness came from a friend of mine whose father used to leave a Post-it Note on the inside of his lunch pail every day. My friend would go to school and open his lunch pail, and he would find a short inspirational message from his father. This brightened his day every single time. Many years later, long after the practice had ended, his father passed away, and I wanted to do something nice for him. One afternoon I sat down with a bunch of Post-it Notes and I wrote dozens of inspirational quotes to try to help him deal with his loss. Then I put them in a little gift box and mailed them to him. When he called to thank me, he was in tears. He said it was the most thoughtful gift he had ever received. This was an eye-opening experience for me. I never imagined that my small act would have such a profound effect on him. Actually, it had a profound effect on both of us, because it taught me that even a tiny kindness can have the impact of a tidal wave.

Kindness tends to be infectious. When you show kindness, you inspire it in others. You pay it forward and fan the flames, and a small act of kindness suddenly takes on a life of its own. If you reach the checkout line at the grocery store at the same time as another person, let that individual go first. If you are driving along in rush-hour traffic and another driver is trying to merge in, slow down and let that other car in. That tiny act of kindness might make that person's day, leading him to share that positive energy with others. Think of the ripple effect! A dozen, maybe even a hundred people, all having a better day because you let a complete stranger get into the checkout line before you. That's what people mean when they say kindness is its own reward.

There's one more story I'd like to share about my father. One day when I was about twelve or thirteen, we were driving along Ventura Boulevard and saw a homeless man huddled in a store doorway. My father stopped the car, opened the trunk, and walked over with a blanket and a pair of shoes. He had a brief exchange with the man, who looked very appreciative, then got back into the car. "Wow," I said, "it's lucky you had that blanket and your old shoes in the trunk of your car. That homeless man looked very pleased."

And my father said, "It wasn't luck. I always keep blankets and my old shoes and used clothing in the trunk of my car, because I know there will be plenty of opportunities to share with people who have less than we do."

I remember I almost wept, but it came from a place of joy. I felt incredibly lucky to have a father who never forgot to count his blessings and who was so considerate of others. I remember thinking, and it's something I think to this day, "If there were more people like my father, the world would be a much nicer place."

Compassion

Compassion is kindness taken to another level. For me, compassion is about being sensitive enough to know that everyone struggles and that you shouldn't stand in judgment. When you work at being uncritical, people respond in a different way. They sense your spiritual generosity.

Everyone is flawed, even you! We are all perfectly imperfect, and people will love you despite—or even because of!—those imperfections. Learn to accept the imperfections. Give people a break and concentrate on your own issues; work every day at becoming a better version of the person you are today.

It hurts to be criticized, as everyone knows from personal experience. For example, I'm not one of those girls who shows a lot of skin, whether on the dance floor or at the beach, and I get criticized about it for all the wrong reasons. Somebody will say that I must not like my body. Or they'll assume that I'm keeping myself covered up because all of my hard work in the gym hasn't yet resulted in six-pack abs. And it's total bullshit, but it can still be hurtful. (Then again, I don't know why I let it hurt me, so I'm working on that.) And I

The best way to cheer yourself up is to try to cheer somebody else up.

—Mark Twain

guess I shouldn't complain, because experiencing how thoughtless people can be with their comments and criticism has made me more thoughtful. I learn a great deal from my own mistakes, but I learn just as much from watching other people make mistakes.

Still, you're not going to get away from criticism. Everyone gets criticized. Heck, Mother Teresa got criticized. And even Jesus got criticized for hanging out with lepers and prostitutes. As Aristotle said, "Criticism is something you can easily avoid by saying nothing, doing nothing, and being nothing." If you don't want to be criticized, you pretty much have to stop living.

Another form of compassion is to stop taking everything so personally. You never really know what's going on inside other people. When they behave badly, you need to understand that it probably has very little to do with you. They're dealing with their own shit and clearly not handling it well, and you shouldn't personalize it. It's not about you; it's about them. If you accept that, you'll be less reactive. And when you're less reactive you make room in your heart for compassion. Remember, be kind. Everyone you meet is fighting a hard battle.

Caitlyn Breaks Her Silence

I actually have a story that speaks to this very issue. It's about my stepdad, Bruce, who not that long ago, for months on end, was stuck in a terrible rut. He had turned into a total Debbie Downer. I remember thinking, *How the hell is he a motivational speaker? He's always in a shitty mood.* Then we found out that he was transitioning, and suddenly his moodiness made perfect sense. Kourtney's partner, Scott, said something that was funny and moving at the same time. "Now I know why you've been such a dick for so many years. Because you've been keeping this to yourself and it's been killing you."

To be honest, I was upset that Bruce hadn't told us about it sooner. And many months later, when Bruce was interviewed by Diane Sawyer, I was even more upset. There were so many things he didn't share with us, things we found out that night, along with 16.9 million other Americans, and that hurt. We were family. Didn't we have a right to know?

In fact, when the Diane Sawyer interview aired, we all gathered at my mother's house to watch it, and I was truly astonished by some of the things I heard. There were so many intimate details he shared with Diane Sawyer, and with the world, that I felt betrayed. He had been a part of my life for twenty-six years, and I thought I deserved more.

On the other hand, it dawned on me that we never fully know other people, even the ones closest to us, and that we often make assumptions or pass judgment based on erroneous information or half-truths. Remember: Hurt people tend to hurt people.

That said, I was guilty of doing the same thing with Bruce. I had lost my father, and now I was losing Bruce. Bruce wanted to be a woman and I could only imagine the battle raging inside his soul. My heart went out to him. But, I saw the transformation as a huge loss.

In some ways I felt the worst part was that other people had known about the transition before we did. I felt devalued by that fact. Bruce had been working behind the scenes with Diane Sawyer and her crew, and he had even been in negotiation with E! about doing his own show, but most of the members of his own family had been kept in the dark. That hurt, and it still hurt when Bruce explained it to me. "Sometimes it's easier to talk about something like this with a complete stranger than it is to share it with your own family," he said.

Oddly enough, we ended up doing a special about the way we handled the news. After we filmed it, I knew that people were never going to understand my reaction. I was still upset and angry. I had not had time to process the news. And even before I saw the footage, I knew I was going to come across as hostile and unpleasant.

Later, however, I was truly happy for Bruce. If this is what he wanted, who was I to tell him he was wrong? He wasn't grumpy anymore, that's for sure! He seemed relieved and genuinely happy. He was about to begin the next chapter of his very unusual life, and it was clear he was excited about it. Caitlyn was finally free! But at the time the show aired, I was still hurting inside. I was losing Bruce, my stepfather. He was becoming another person. And I felt he hadn't given me enough time to say good-bye. Did I blame him? Did I think he'd been unfair? For about a minute, yes. But then I remembered more wise words from Richard Carlson in *Don't Sweat the Small Stuff* . . . : "One of the mistakes many of us make is that we feel sorry for ourselves, or for others, thinking that life *should* be fair, or that someday it will be. It's not and it won't. When we make this mistake we tend to spend a lot of time wallowing and/or complaining about what's wrong with life. . . . 'It's not fair,' we complain, not realizing that, perhaps, it was never intended to be."

When the family special aired, it was all there, in my words and in my eyes. The pain and anger and hostility. When I get emotional, I get *very* emotional, and maybe I was too passionate and too vocal, but it was real; it was what I felt. It was my truth without the benefit of distance; it was truth unedited.

I want people to understand. This was not about Bruce transitioning into a woman; it was his decision and he had been struggling with it for a long time and I was happy that he had found the answer. It was about my own loss; it was about the pain I felt because he was walking out of our lives.

Later Bruce was completely open with us about everything. He was relieved that he could finally tell us and that he didn't have to keep the secret to himself. But even then he had to do it in front of the camera crew and the producers and all sorts of people, because they provided a sort of safety net for him simply by being there. It's like if you're breaking up with someone it's easier to do it in a restaurant because there's less likelihood that he or she will make a scene in public.

But the message from Bruce was loud and clear. He basically said, "I am sixty-five years old. If tomorrow I was diagnosed with cancer and told I would not have time to transition, I would regret it for the remainder of my short life. It really means that much to me, and I ask for your support because I am going through with it."

There are two reasons I'm sharing this story. One is to illustrate the fact that you never really know other people and therefore you should never stand in judgment. And the other goes back to something that I touched on earlier, about the importance of controlling your response to even the most challenging situations. I don't think I responded badly to Bruce's transformation, because I was deeply hurt, but I do think I was wrong to let my anger get the better of me, and for that I am genuinely sorry.

Plus the anger didn't do anyone any good. Quite the contrary. Somebody once said that being angry is like holding a hot coal in your hand, and that's absolutely right. When you hold on to anger, the only person you're burning is yourself.

I got caught up in the emotion. It happens to all of us, and there will be times when it happens to me again. But I processed my feelings and got through it, and when I came out on the other side, I did so with a stronger, more understanding heart. And really, when you think about it, that's not a bad result.

Also, the experience made me think about something that had happened many years earlier, when my father was dying. One day, while he was in the midst of saying his good-byes, he sent for Bruce. Bruce went to see him, and my father told him, "I feel very comfortable leaving my kids with you. You have been a terrific second father to them. It gives me comfort knowing that they are in such good hands. Promise me you will always take good care of them." Afterward, he told us kids how much he appreciated Bruce. "You have a stepdad who really loves you and treats you as if you were his own. I just want to make sure you appreciate it and that you keep him in your prayers."

I still get choked up when I think about that. Even on his deathbed, my father was doing his best to offer us a little guidance in this uncertain world.

Nowadays, whenever I'm with Caitlyn, there are times when I feel like crying with happiness. She's free. Never in my life have I been witness to such a monumental transformation. Caitlyn has been released from a prison not of her own making. In her mind, for years now, she's been saying, "I'm not this person. I don't want to be this person. I know I have the soul of a woman." And to me that level of self-acceptance is a truly beautiful thing. It is the ultimate source of strength. It's as if Caitlyn finally said, "I need to be who I want to be, and I have to be honest, and I just hope that other people will accept me."

And you know what? People accepted. And *more* than accepted: They rejoiced and praised her!

In the heat of emotion, I briefly lost my way, but who doesn't make mistakes? Looking back, I realize I need to work on my empathy. It's important to be kind, not just to family but to the people in the world around you. We're all gimping along trying to find our way, trying to better ourselves, and if we can learn to exhibit a little empathy, that shows true strength of heart.

Life Is *Not* a Competition

When I was in my early twenties, I used to think life was a competition, but now I want everyone to win. We all have our own definition of success, so there's plenty of room at the top. Another person's success doesn't diminish my own. On the contrary, it makes the world one person happier, and that's got to be good for all of us, right?

When I figured this out, I came up with a mantra of my very own: *I am more than enough.* And damn it, it's true! I *am* more than enough. I know myself and like myself, despite my weaknesses and flaws, and while I know I'll never be perfect, I'm going to keep trying. There is no such thing as perfect. Nobody attains perfection. But if you keep working at it, you grow and evolve, and to me that's sort of the point: to be a better person today than I was yesterday; to become the best possible version of myself.

I also know that nothing happens overnight, not in the gym and not in my heart. Things that take longer tend to last longer, because you did them right.

For example, I used to react to things very quickly, without thinking. It made me seem hotheaded, and sometimes I still am a little hotheaded, and I don't like that about myself, so I'm working on that. I guess you could say I'm exercising that part of my personality. (You could also say I'm *exorcising* it, but let's not go there.) Now I try to

Comparison
is the thief
of joy.

—Theodore Roosevelt

think before I speak, and even if I don't always succeed, I'm definitely showing improvement. I actually learned something about this from watching my little sister Kylie, who is only seventeen. When she sits down for an interview, she really takes time to consider her responses to questions, and she always answers in a thoughtful manner. I used to not be able to do this. If a reporter came to see me and I knew we had only ten minutes for the interview, I would try to be nice by answering quickly and talking fast and trying to give him or her as much "good" material as possible. But as I've become an emotionally stronger person, I've come to realize that one short, thoughtful, honest sentence is better than a page full of platitudes, and that thoughtfulness gets results. Slowing down is great. Slowing down can also save you a lot of trouble and pain in the long run. You don't want to make a permanent decision in response to a temporary emotion.

Mannerisms also come into play. I tend to talk with my hands, gesticulating a little wildly at times, and I came to realize that some people found this behavior aggressive. So I began working on that, too. In fact, from time to time, I would literally sit on my hands to make sure that the person I was talking to didn't get the mistaken impression that I was being combative. It sounds a little crazy, I know, but it works.

Sometimes I *do* feel a little combative and aggressive, and in recent years I've started figuring out how to deal with that, too. In the past, I would just get bitchy or irritable—and occasionally I still do—but recently I've learned to short-circuit the feeling by taking a few minutes for myself. I have no problem telling people that I need a little alone time, and people have no problem giving it to me. But I'm not perfect, and it doesn't always work out as planned. Sometimes I *am* a bitch, and I'm not proud of it, but I try to be an honest bitch.

Think Before You Act

If somebody does something to hurt me or to piss me off, I want to get it off my chest. In the old days, if somebody said "Fuck you" to me, I'd say "Fuck you" right back. But that's neither useful nor productive. That was my alter ego, Khlo-Money or K-Money, speaking. That was the Khloé who would put up her fists at the drop of a hat, ready to fight her battles (along with everybody's else's). But Khlo-Money doesn't come around much anymore. The new Khloé is stronger than her; the new Khloé has more control. There will always be times when I get hotheaded or lose my temper, because that's part of who I am. The other day, for example, somebody tweeted something about Lamar that was wrong, stupid, and meanspirited. I immediately picked up my phone to tweet back, and I was angry, but before I sent the tweet I actually managed to stop myself. I realized that my angry response wasn't going to do anyone any good, me least of all, so I didn't send it. I was proud of myself, and I find myself doing that kind of thing more and more lately. For example, I'll get upset about something, so I'll park myself in front of my laptop and write an angry email to the guilty party. Then I won't send it right away. It's written, and I leave it in my draft folder; an hour or two later I'll reread it. If I still feel the same way, I'll send it. But more often that not, the feeling will have passed and I will delete the draft and get on with my life.

A related issue is the tendency most of us have to blame circumstances on the people around us. You blame your parents, your boss, your best friend, your lover. And even if from time to time you're right—if it really *was* his or her fault—blaming others doesn't change the situation. Only you can change the situation, so what good does blaming do?

I know this guy who had a really mean, creepy father. The man was abusive and couldn't treat people decently. By the time he reached middle age, he had driven everyone away with his unpleas-antness and anger. And when my friend was still an impressionable young kid, his father used to tell him, "You're going to be just like me when you grow up. It's in your genes. You'll be short-tempered and unpredictable. You'll have no friends. People won't like you."

Well, my friend thought about what his father had said—obviously it made a huge, scary impression on him—and he wondered whether he might in fact be genetically predisposed toward that type of be-havior. So growing up, he made an effort to be as different from his father as possible, and he succeeded beyond his wildest expectations. Today he lives in a penthouse condo in Santa Monica. He has a beau-tiful girlfriend. And he spends all of his free time rescuing animals.

When I asked him how he did it, he said, "It was easy. Every other day, my father would tell me I was going to be just like him, and I was young and vulnerable, and I began to believe it. But one day I decided I would do everything in my power to *not* be like him, to be the opposite, and it worked."

I love that story. My friend decided he didn't want to be a victim of genetics or of his environment growing up, and he realized he had the power to find his way out. But he could just as easily have turned into a creep, and spent the rest of his life blaming his father.

The Art of Prayer

When I was growing up, we used to go to church every Sunday and to Bible study every Wednesday. Later we stopped going, but my father would visit each of our rooms every night, to see how we were doing.

Buddhist mindfulness is about the present, but I also think it's about being real. Being awake to everything. Feeling like nothing can hurt you if you can look it straight on.

—Krista Tippett

These visits were a form of prayer. He guided our conversations so that we became aware that our lives were full of blessings. He would begin by thanking me—"I am really glad you helped me with the garden this afternoon"—and then he would ask me about the rest of my day. How were things going at school? Did I have anything on my mind? Did I need anything from him? Amazingly, he was always able to turn every negative into a positive. If I didn't do well on a test, for example, he assured me that I would do better next time. If the popular girls at school didn't want to be friends with me, it was their loss. These nightly conversations always ended the same way. My father would say, "Give me a hug." And after we hugged, he'd say, "Now we have a wall of protection around us."

This was the way my father prayed with us. It was a conversation, but at a higher level, and every night I looked forward to those conversations with my father. He made me feel loved and safe, and beyond that, he made me understand the meaning of the word *gratitude*. Life was a huge gift, he always reminded me. Live it wisely.

I still pray every night before I go to bed. Then I try to read a little, usually something inspirational—I like books by Joel Osteen—and after I turn out the light I have a conversation with my father. I know he's there and he's listening, and just saying hello and chatting about my day makes me feel good inside. I keep my father close to my heart.

The Future

When I think about the future, I definitely see myself married, and with plenty of kids running around. That's who I am and what I want and I know it will come about.

When your marriage fails, it's a lousy feeling, but this doesn't mean you're a failure. The marriage failed, period. Dust yourself off and learn from it and move on. It was especially hard for me because I've never believed in divorce, and I still don't. When people marry, they should believe in their hearts that it's going to last forever. To believe less is to try less, and this is not a good way to start.

I have a number of girlfriends who've also been through divorce, and they've all survived it. Some of them have already moved on to new relationships, and some have sworn that they'll never fall in love again. I understand both extremes. I fall somewhere in the middle. I don't need a man, but I am certainly not bitter. I loved being married, being part of a team, and I know it will happen again. But I'm not in a hurry. When the right one comes along, I'll know.

One of my favorite quotes is "You can't love someone into loving you." I know this from experience. No matter how much you love someone, no matter how much of yourself you give, if that other person doesn't feel it, it's not happening. Stop chasing him or her. The right one will come along.

Since my marriage ended, I have been enjoying a time of tremendous growth. I really don't mind being alone. I know so many people, particularly in the arts and entertainment, who simply can't stand to be alone. Even their entourages have entourages! And I don't understand that. We all need quiet time, time to be alone with our thoughts. If you can't learn to enjoy your own company, you'll never really get to know yourself.

My goal is to be *happy*. I know there will be periods of happiness and periods of unhappiness, and like it or not, I will have to live with both. But, my goal is to live a rich, interesting, productive, generous, kind, mindful life full of love.

Acknowledgments

There are so many people who helped me along this journey—thank you all for your loyalty, your endless love, your generosity, and your overwhelming support.

Endless thanks to my family. You are my heart and happiness. Thanks to Mom whose wisdom, strength, love, and support has made me who I am, and for her close read, which helped bring the book home. I love you Mama. To Kourtney, Kimberly, Rob, Kendall, and Kylie who help me be the best version of myself, who make me laugh, who fill my heart with peace, and keep me strong at my lowest points. To all my nieces and nephews, thanks for giving me the purest form of love and laughter. Thank you to Caitlyn for showing me how to be true to myself.

Thank you to Lamar for giving me some of the best years of my life and for everything you taught me about being strong. Before I met you I felt invisible, and after I felt seen.

Thank you to my best friends Malika and Khadijah who were with me every step of the way. The secret-keepers to my life, they are the ones who pass no judgment but only give love.

Thank you to my glam squad/therapists/besties—Jen Atkin, Joyce Bonelli, Clyde Haygood, and Rob Scheppy—for your loyalty and for your protection of my heart. And for enduring my mood swings.

Thanks to Cynthia Bussey who brings me joy in a thousand different ways. Cici you have no idea the positive impact you have on my life. To Alexa Okyle and Sydney Hitchcock, who smooth the way every single day.

I'm indebted to Philip Goglia for teaching me how to fuel a healthy body, to Brad Johnson for being a spiritual beacon, and to Gunnar Peterson for helping me build my strength—physically and mentally—and for giving me the confidence I never thought I could have. I'm forever grateful!!!

Many thanks to all the people at William Morris Endeavor who have been so supportive, and special thanks to Mel Berger, who is a calming force, and Lance Klein, who is a tireless advocate for me. Thanks too, to the ladies at 42 West, Holly Shakoor Fleischer and Carrie Gordon. Thank you to Steven Gomillion for his amazing photographs and to Alice Bamford and Ann Eysenring of One Gun Ranch for opening their home to us for the photo shoot.

I'm so grateful to Pablo Fenjves who helped me not only to find my voice, but also helped me write a book that captures my spirit and my heart, and to Alexis Gargagliano, my editor, who helped bring the book to life—on the page and in the world. The entire Regan Arts team has been wonderful to work with. Judith Regan is visionary and made this book a reality. Richard Ljoenes created the gorgeous cover, Nancy Singer made every page beautiful, and so many other creative, talented people helped get the book into the world—Kurt Andrews, Mia Abrahams, Lynne Ciccaglione, and John Ekizian.

Big thanks to my fans for all your support. You are an inspiration.

IMAGE CREDITS

Steven Gomillion, ii, Photo Insert; Courtesy of the author, vi, viii, xi, xiii, xiv, xvii, xx, 2, 6, 8, 16, 18, 38, 47, 49, 53, 58, 67, 85, 107, 110, 112, 116, 119, 129, 133, 138, 140, 144, 154, 157, 162, 175, 176, 192, 194; © Brock Miller/Splash News/Corbis, 32; Dave Lee/Getty Images, 33; ©ImageCollect.com/StarMaxWorldwide, 52; © 2010 Phil Ramey/RameyPix/Corbis, 72; Frazer Harrison/GettyImages, 73; Tinseltown/Shutterstock.com, 78; David Becker/Getty Images, 79.

About the Author

Khloé Kardashian is a *New York Times* bestselling author and star of the E! Network number one hit show, *Keeping Up with the Kardashians*. She has also starred in *Kourtney and Khloé take Miami*, *Khloé and Lamar*, *Kourtney and Khloé Take The Hamptons*, *Celebrity Apprentice*, and *The X-Factor*, among many other shows. She is also the host of the new talk show *Kocktails With Khloé*. Khloé is an accomplished entrepreneur who, along with her sisters, owns her own clothing line, Kardashian Collection, hair care line, Kardashian Beauty, kids' line, Kardashian Kids, and her own DASH boutiques around the country. She is also executive producer of *DASH Dolls*, the sixth series installment of the franchise. She lives in Los Angeles.